# Contents

# Introduction

Dublin is a city of threes. It has three castles on its coat of arms, and it has three Gaelic names: Dubhlinne, the black or the dark river pool; Baile Atha Cliath — Baile the town and Atha Cliath the Hurdle Ford; and Druim Cuill Coillte — Druim the ridge and Cuill Coillte the hazel wood.

The three sides of the people of Dublin are friendship, good humour and colourful speech. Dubliners love visitors, because visitors ask questions and Dubliners love talking. Brendan Behan used to say that Dubliners spend words like sailors. Another good point about true Dubliners is that if they don't know the answer to your question, they will stop someone else to ask it, and then repeat the answer to you adding their little comment in their own special flavour and colour.

Dublin is a warm city. It has a triangle of colours, Georgian russet red, battleship grey and Liffey green. These colours are on its courts, churches, and the Custom House with its long room and its statue of Lady Hope looking down the River Liffey as it flows in and out of Dublin Bay.

Outside the city are mountains covered with primroses and comlechs. When we were young we used to head for the Three-Rock Mountain, otherwise known as Slieve Rua, the 'red mountain'. We were never short of a mountain to explore — Kilmashogue, Tibradden, Glendoo Mountain across Glencullen Valley, Cruagh, Kilakee, and Mont Pelier, each of them with ghosts, leprechauns, wild flowers, green ferns, sparkling streams and a magnificent view of the city.

An easier way to have the whole of Dublin Bay before you is to travel by DART — Dublin Area Rapid Transit. North to Howth Head and the Marina Village, south to Bray Head and the seaside towns of County Wicklow, this new railway with its green trains has won the hearts of Dubliners.

Dublin is a city to enjoy, where there is always something to do or some place to go . . . . the Phoenix Park, the National Gallery, the treasures of the Irish Nation in the National Museum. Or a picnic in the mountains, or merely a walk through the streets smelling the yeast and the hops up around St James's Gate Brewery, or the combined scents of Moore Street with its flowers, fruit, vegetables and meats, or Bewley's shops when they grind and brew the coffee . . .

This is Dublin — my home sweet home.

ÉAMONN MacTHOMÁIS
*A bard of Dublin for the 20th century, Éamonn MacThomáis has written several books and made over 20 films on the city, where he has always lived.*

# *Pocket Guide to*
# DUBLIN

**AA**

Published by The Automobile Association,
Fanum House, Basingstoke, Hampshire RG21 2EA

**Illustrations:** Alan Roe

**Editorial contributors:** Pat Liddy (Walks); Adrian MacLoughlin (City Centre); Séamus MacMathúna (Traditional Music); Charles Nelson (Gardens of Dublin County); David Norris (Georgian Houses, Literary Dublin); Kathy Sheridan (Directory); Peter Somerville-Large (A Thousand Years and More).

**Second edition prepared by Lyn Gallagher.**

The assistance of Dublin & East Tourism and Bord Fáilte is gratefully acknowledged.

**Maps and Plans** produced by the cartographic Department of the Automobile Association

**Filmsetting by** Servis Filmsetting Ltd, Manchester.

**Printed and bound by** Grosvenor Press (Portsmouth) Ltd.

**ISBN 0 7490 455 2**

Published by The Automobile Association, Fanum House, Basingstoke, Hampshire RG21 2EA

# About this Book

**Dublin City Guide,** designed to be the complete guide for tourist or resident, contains the following sections.

City Plan
Large-scale map of the City Centre, with a street index and places of interest clearly shown.

Features
Written by local experts, these introductory articles cover subjects of special importance in the city — its literary connections, its remarkable Georgian architecture and over a thousand years of history. Also covered in this section are traditional Irish music, which can be heard at numerous places in the city, and gardens to visit both in Dublin and in the surrounding countryside.

City Centre: Places to Visit
Here places of interest, listed alphabetically, are described in detail. Each entry includes its street name, so it can easily be located on the street plan on page 6. For opening times and practical information refer to the Directory.

City Walks
Six walks, with step-by-step route directions, have been carefully planned to take in the best of the city. A clear, easy-to-follow map accompanies each walk. The chief places of interest along the way are described in the text, and these are keyed to the maps by numbers.

Directory
Seventeen pages packed with useful information grouped into sections (see page 74). All you need to know about where to eat and stay, recreation, shops, sports and services, plus useful addresses and opening times for all the places of interest described in the book. A calendar of events lists the major annual festivals, shows and sporting events month by month.

# Key to Town Plan

| | |
|---|---|
| AA Recommended roads | ▬ |
| Restricted roads | ▬ ▬ ▬ |
| Buildings of interest | Station ▢ |
| Churches | † |
| Car Parks | ▣ |
| Parks and open spaces | ▨ |
| Insurance shop | AA |

# Key to Places of Interest

| | |
|---|---|
| 1 Abbey Presbyterian Church | D8 |
| 2 Abbey Theatre | E7 |
| 3 Aldborough House | F8 |
| 4 Bank of Ireland | D6 |
| 5 Belvedere House | C8 |
| 6 Bluecoat School | A6 |
| 7 Brazen Head | A6 |
| 8 Casino, Marino | F8 |
| 9 Chester Beatty Library | F4 |
| 10 Christ Church Cathedral | B5 |
| 11 City Hall | C5 |
| 12 Custom House | E7 |
| 13 Dublin Castle | C5 |
| 14 Dublin Civic Museum | D5 |
| 15 Dublin Writers Museum | C8 |
| 16 Eccles Street | C8 |
| 17 Fitzwilliam Square | F3 |
| 18 Four Courts | B6 |
| 19 Gaiety Theatre | D4 |
| 20 Gate Theatre | D8 |
| 21 General Post Office | D7 |
| 22 Government Buildings | E4 |
| 23 Grand Canal | A1-F2 |
| 24 Guinness Brewery | A5 |
| 25 Heraldic Museum | E4 |
| 26 Iveagh House | D3 |
| 27 Kilmainham Gaol | A5 |
| 28 King's Inns | B8 |
| 29 Leinster House | E4 |
| 30 Mansion House | D4 |
| 31 Marsh's Library | B4 |
| 32 Mountjoy Square | E8 |
| 33 Municipal Gallery of Modern Art | C8 |
| 34 Museum of Childhood | C1 |
| 35 National Botanic Gardens | B8 |
| 36 National Gallery of Ireland | E4 |
| 37 National Library | E4 |
| 38 National Museum | E4 |
| 39 Natural History Museum | E4 |
| 40 Newman House | D3 |
| 41 Olympia Theatre | C5 |
| 42 Phoenix Park | A6 |
| 43 Powerscourt House | D5 |
| 44 Pro-Cathedral (St Mary's) | D7 |
| 45 Prospect Cemetery | B8 |
| 46 Rathfarnham Castle | A1 |
| 47 Rotunda Hospital | D8 |
| 48 Royal Canal | C8 |
| 49 Royal College of Surgeons | D4 |
| 50 Royal Dublin Society | F4 |
| 51 Royal Hospital, Kilmainham | A5 |
| 52 St Andrew's Church | D5 |
| 53 St Ann's Church | D4 |
| 54 St Audoen's Churches | B5 |
| 55 St Catherine's Church | A5 |
| 56 St Francis Xavier Church | E8 |
| 57 St George's Church | C8 |
| 58 St Mary's Abbey | C7 |
| 59 St Mary's Church | C7 |
| 60 St Michan's Church | B6 |
| 61 St Patrick's Cathedral | B4 |
| 62 St Werburgh's Church | C5 |
| 63 Tailors' Hall | B5 |
| 64 Temple Bar | C6-D6 |
| 65 Trinity College | E5 |
| 66 Tyrone House | D7 |
| 67 University Church | D3 |
| 68 University College, National Concert Hall | D2 |

# Street Index with Grid Reference

## Central Dublin

Pocket Guide to DUBLIN

# FEATURES

Historical, architectural and cultural
background

# A Thousand Years & More

*D**ublin, originally an ecclesiastical settlement, and then in turn a Viking raiding and trading base, a Norman stronghold, the British Empire's second city and capital of an independent state, is steeped in tragic and glorious history.*

**DUBLIN DATA**

**The Millennium** celebrations of 1988 were inspired by Mael Sechnaill's capture of the city in AD988.
**Handel** conducted the first performance of the *Messiah* in Fishamble Street, Dublin, 1742.
**The Guinness Brewery** in Dublin is the world's largest producer of stout.
**A Dublin lion**, from the Phoenix Park Zoo, went on to become the lion of the MGM films.

Dublin is generally considered a Viking creation – a Norse community older than Oslo or Bergen. But long before the arrival of the Vikings, people lived around the protected waters of Dublin Bay. Here Larnian hunters and fishermen kept dogs as domestic animals 5,000 years ago, and ate oxen, sheep and pigs. Neolithic farmers built their tombs at the foot of the Dublin mountains, and a community of Beaker Folk (called after their pottery) flourished in the Bronze Age.

With the coming of Christianity a spread of monasteries and hermit cells appeared north and south of the Liffey. Along the Poddle, the Liffey's tributary, stood four churches, St Patrick on its island, St Brigid, St Kevin and St MacTaill, which are assumed to be Celtic foundations. The original small settlement was named Ath Cliath, 'ford of hurdles' and was at a crossroads. Below the steep ridge on which stood the Church of St Columcille, later replaced by St Audoen, the Poddle met the Liffey, forming a pool – Linn Dubh, the Black Pool.

Vikings had been plundering the east coast of Ireland for decades. Then in the summer of AD837, 65 longboats sailed down from Scotland and Orkney. The traditional site of their Dublin has been confirmed by archaeology. Excavations around Christ Church have revealed the remains of post and wattle houses, and the detritus of the new town: fragments of Viking clothes and jewellery, bones of eaten animals, combs in their hundreds. The Battle of Dublin in December AD919 ensured the Viking settlement. Ireland temporarily united against the Vikings in the 11th century, who were routed at Clontarf in the greatest battle in early Irish history, on Good Friday, 23 April 1014.

Political unity did not last however, and appeals were made to Henry II of England for help. Thus began the Norman invasion of Ireland which culminated in Henry II's landing in 1171 and his assumption for the English crown of the Lordship of Ireland. He kept Dublin and its environs – the Pale – for himself.

The Normans were great builders. Apart from what survives in stone, part of the city wall, the cathedrals of St Patrick and Christ Church, Dublin Castle, the grim seat of government, and various churches and tombs, the most vivid reminders of the Norman presence are surviving street names: Bull Alley, Golden Lane, Cornmarket, High Street, Winetavern Street, Fishamble Street.

In spite of raids from Irishmen in the surrounding hills, a failed attempt to create a Celtic kingdom, siege, fire, and pestilence as the Black Death brought its devastation, medieval Dublin enlarged and grew more prosperous. A line of 12th-century warehouses excavated at Wood Quay indicates the importance of trade with Europe. Surviving assembly rolls and guild charters, descriptions of religious festivals, guild ceremonies and other events give clues to the life of the city. The new merchant class flourished, while the records of the Priory of the Holy Trinity provide evidence of a comfortable lifestyle for clergy and monks.

Silken Thomas's rebellion in 1534 heralded the demise of medieval Dublin. In the period between the accession of Henry VIII as King of Ireland in 1536, and the death of Queen Elizabeth in 1601, the Reformation made its impact on the city, while the savage surrounding conflict, culminating in the defeat of Gaelic Ireland, strengthened the capital which became the main base of English operations against the Irish. The wave of new English settlers encouraged the impact of the Renaissance, and Trinity College, a counterblast to Popery, was founded in 1592 on land confiscated from the Priory of All Hallows.

In the early part of the following century, dissent and civil war shrivelled Dublin to a wretched state. But after the constraints of the Commonwealth came the Restoration and Ormonde's viceroyalty, bringing increased trade. The city underwent a great architectural expansion. With a rising population, houses began to spill out beyond the old confines. By the end of the 17th century, Dublin was a flourishing commercial centre. During the following century it was transformed into one of the handsomest of Georgian cities, so that today it is hard for the visitor to ignore the influence of the 18th century. The beautiful rose-coloured brick terraces, elegant mansions, wide streets and squares made up one of Europe's finest capitals. But the century of Dean Swift, Lord Charlemont, Sheridan and the rest, was also a period of political agitation when the sufferings of the poor provided a perpetual contrast. In Malton's *Picturesque and Descriptive Views of the City of Dublin*, a beggar is usually present.

The age of elegance was brought to an end by a wave of political unrest, which erupted in the uprising by the United Irishmen in 1798. The rebellion was crushed by English armies, the Act of Union was established, and the fortunes of the city began to wane. During the 19th century the railway took over from the canal and the first horsedrawn tram made its way down Sackville Street. It was an age of great upheaval, with Daniel O'Connell's massive meetings inspiring cries for Repeal, and Parnell and Davitt fuelling the campaign for Home Rule. Catholic emancipation in 1829, by which time Catholics formed over 70 per cent of the population, helped the rise of a new professional class. But poverty was also increasing, and the Dublin slums were among the worst in Europe.

The end of the old order began with the Easter Rising of 1916 which was fought in Dublin's streets. When Civil War broke out in June 1922, shelling destroyed much more of the city, but the GPO and other public buildings were later restored.

The Dublin that slowly emerged from the ashes of conflict touches our own age. Only a proportion of the elegant Georgian buildings survive, but much of the warm intimacy of Dublin life seems to survive in its spacious streets and handsome squares.

ST AUDOEN'S ARCH

## Georgian Houses

*W*ide, spacious streets and harmonious *Georgian terraces make Dublin one of Europe's most beautiful cities. A close look at the terrace façades reveals a wealth of decorative detail, in fanlights, door knockers and even coal hole covers, while within are nobly proportioned rooms and gloriously exuberant plasterwork.*

Dublin enjoys a superb natural location sheltered by the Dublin Mountains, watered by the River Liffey, the arms of the Bay reaching out as if in welcome to the traveller, so that it is not surprising that for a thousand years and more it has been a major centre of habitation. Little trace remains, however, of its medieval origin, apart from the line of some of the oldest streets and the two great cathedrals, Christ Church and St Patrick's (and even St Patrick's derives its principal international celebrity from association with the iconoclastic 18th-century writer Dean Jonathan Swift). To most people the essential spirit of Dublin, especially as expressed in architecture, is that of the 18th century. During that period Dublin, although governed as was the rest of the island by a Protestant Ascendancy, was the seat of an independent parliament under the British crown, second city of what was fast becoming an empire and the self-styled seventh city of Christendom. The confidence of the age is reflected in the great public buildings created by the genius of architects like James Gandon, Thomas Ivory and Francis Johnston. Dublin's skyline is still dominated by such impressive works as the Royal Hospital Kilmainham, now magnificently restored, the Bluecoat School, the façade of Trinity College, the Custom House, the Four Courts, the Parliament House (now the Bank of Ireland, College Green) and the King's Inns in Henrietta Street. Apart from these magnificent places of public and professional resort, the domestic buildings of Georgian Dublin continued into the private sphere the ideals of harmony and balance, regularity and symmetry so dear to 18th-century classicism.

DETAIL FROM CUSTOM HOUSE

## WIDE AND CONVENIENT STREETS

Nor was the coherent development of the capital left to the whim of individual taste, and Dubliners still have cause to be grateful to the 'Commissioners for Making Wide and Convenient Streets', known popularly as the Wide Street Commissioners. This influential body was established by an Act of 1757 and given the power to acquire and demolish unsatisfactory, dilapidated or inconvenient buildings, and to lay down strict standards governing the architectural character of new buildings which replaced them. They were also empowered to compensate individual builders for any additional expense incurred in meeting these standards. Among the streets to benefit from their attentions were Lower Sackville (now O'Connell) Street, Westmoreland Street, D'Olier Street, Dame Street and Rutland (now Parnell) Square. In 1773 a parallel body, the Paving Board, was set up to oversee the 'paving cleansing lighting draining and improving' of the city's streets. By the last quarter of the 18th century, Dublin was what Paris was to become only later under Napoleon, an elegant city of planned and luxuriously broad thoroughfares.

It was a compact city of less than 200,000 souls, lying entirely between the two canals – the Grand to the south of the city with its graceful locks and bridges such as the Huband Bridge (1791) at Percy Place, and the plainer, more straightforward Royal Canal on the north side. Indeed the keen observer can still clearly note the limits of the Georgian city in the stylistic change that occurs as the tidemark of Victoriana washes against it. The contrast between the mellow, honey-tinged Georgian brick and its heavier, more aggressively red Victorian counterpart is quite marked at points such as the junction of Belvedere Place and the North Circular Road on the north side, or at the meeting of Lower Mount Street and Northumberland Road on the south. It must be acknowledged however that Mount Street has now been almost totally destroyed and its original buildings recently replaced by high and unimaginative office blocks, while many of the imposing Victorian residences of Northumberland Road have completed the initial stages of transition to the commercial sector.

## FROZEN IN TIME

Within its two canals central Dublin remained frozen in time, an almost totally intact Georgian anachronism until a sudden boom in property speculation in the early 1960s led to an unexpected and unparalleled devastation. Shamefully the signal for destruction was first given by a State agency – the Electricity Supply Board – which despite public protest pulled down 26 Georgian houses and set in their place a jarring modern office block, effectively destroying what had been the longest continuous Georgian vista in Europe – the view from Holles Street past Merrion Square and Fitzwilliam Square to the Dublin Mountains. In fact by the mid-1960s the core of Dublin had become vulnerable for a variety of reasons. The great houses of the nobility, set in splendid isolation, like Leinster, Tyrone, Aldborough, Powerscourt and Charlemont Houses, or in serried ranks along the streets and squares of the inner city, had been rapidly

**PARLIAMENT HOUSE**

*Tell us what the pile contains? Many a head that holds no brains* wrote Swift of the building that is now the Bank or Ireland but once housed Parliament.

drained of their aristocratic occupants with the passing of the Act of Union in 1800, which abolished the independent Dublin Parliament. Throughout the 19th century the glory of the old mansions faded as they passed from the aristocracy into the hands of first the professional classes, then to merchants and tradespeople and ultimately into subdivision into tenements. This situation was compounded by the freezing of tenement rents during World War I, to avoid mutinous murmurings from the families of those at the front, and the problem thus created was left unresolved for 60 years after the war's end. This meant that rents became so uneconomic that non-resident landlords either refused or could not afford to carry out essential repairs. In addition, many officials of the New State established at the beginning of the 1920s felt alienated from this part of their heritage, seeing in Georgian Dublin merely the expendable remnant of an arrogant, exploitative and alien ruling class. Nowadays, happily, this phase has passed and the preservation of the best of what remains of Georgian Dublin is supported by all sectors, who appreciate that what is valued is not the pretensions of the past but the surviving work of Irish artists, craftsmen builders and 'stuccodores' – men like Charles Thorp, Francis Ryan, Michael Stapleton and Robert West.

## WHAT TO LOOK FOR

**Door cases** in a rich variety of styles. **Door knockers** shaped as human heads or animals, and delicately patterned **fanlights** above the doors. **Windows** divided by glazing bars into small squares. Ornate **foot scrapers**, **brackets** for lanterns, and **coal hole covers**. At dusk, look up for glimpses of exuberantly decorated **ceilings**.

## GEORGIAN TOWN HOUSES

The typical pattern of the Georgian town house is that of a red brick, four-storey over basement construction, with a pitched and slated roof, granite steps to the hall door and a basement area protected by wrought- or cast-iron railings. An attractive feature of these houses was the division of the windows into small squares by glazing bars, and the delicately graceful leaded fanlights over the hall door, although sadly these have both been replaced over the years in some houses by plain glass. The apparent uniformity of the brick façade and the regularity of the roofline in a streetscape can mislead the casual observer into ignoring the subtle variation in detail. There is in fact a surprising variety of door cases, and the sharp eyed will enjoy the range of imagination displayed in items such as door knockers in the guise of human heads or animal forms, the differing shapes of foot scrapers, the individualistic patterns of leaves, spirals or geometrical arabesques decorating even the humble cast-iron coal hole covers inserted into the granite paving sets. Here and there on the railings can be found the remains of the standard brackets which once held candle- or oil-lit lanterns, a relic of the 17th-century ordinance under which every fifth house was obliged to provide lighting for the public footpath.

The real magnificence of these houses only becomes apparent when one penetrates behind the somewhat restrained façades. The noble proportions of high-ceilinged rooms are pleasing in themselves, but the great glory of Dublin lies in the unique lightness and exuberance of the plasterwork decoration on ceilings, friezes and walls. A small number of private houses are open to the public on a limited basis and a list of these may be obtained from the offices of Dublin Tourism in O'Connell Street.

## AROUND THE STREETS

A favourite pastime of Dublin antiquarians is 'ceiling spotting'. This is best done at dusk when the lights are on in the first floor reception rooms, and the stroller can enjoy from a safe vantage point on the pavement the tracery of 18th-century plasterwork, often picked out in delicate pastel shades. The area around Merrion Square, Fitzwilliam Square and St Stephen's Green is a particularly rich location for this hobby. The squares themselves were originally for the private enjoyment of the residents, but in St Stephen's Green, Merrion Square and Mountjoy Square, Dublin Corporation Parks Department now maintain well-tended public pleasure gardens. The most recently opened of these, Merrion Square, is a particular delight in which it is possible to refresh the weary spirit in the mellow ambience of the past and relish the full impact of the surrounding buildings away from the roar of the traffic. Number 73 Merrion Square, finely restored, is the headquarters of the Irish Architectural Archive and houses a unique collection of photographs, plans and architectural drawings.

Although there is now considerable modern intrusion into St Stephen's Green, some fine 18th-century houses do remain, notably No 86, originally the home of Burnchapel Whaley and his son Buck Whaley who won a bet by walking to Jerusalem and playing handball against its walls. This subsequently became part of University College Dublin, and the setting for a number of celebrated scenes in the novels of James Joyce, its most distinguished graduate. Number 85 next door has a very fine ceiling in the saloon by Francini. On the same side is the imposing Iveagh House, remodelled by Sir Benjamin Guinness and presented to the nation by the 2nd Earl of Iveagh, also a member of the brewing family, in 1939. It now houses the Department of Foreign Affairs and provides a glorious background for state dinners.

Just off the Green are three superb houses: Ely House, Northland House and Powerscourt House. Ely House is in Ely Place facing down Hume Street towards the Green. The plasterwork here is by Michael Stapleton, and one of the unusual features of the house is a beautiful wrought-iron staircase with panels depicting the labours of

*ELY HOUSE STAIRCASE DETAIL*

### PLASTERWORK

The great 18th-century 'stuccodores' (or plasterworkers) moulded the wet plaster on the wall or ceiling itself to create their exquisite decorations. Later, plasterwork was made in moulds and applied to the surface when set.

Hercules. At the beginning of the century this was the residence of the surgeon Sir Thornley Stoker, brother of Bram Stoker, author of *Dracula*. It is now the headquarters of the Knights of Columbanus, a conservative Roman Catholic organisation. Northland House, No 19 Dawson Street, has been the home of the Royal Irish Academy since the middle of the last century, and is remarkable for its rococo plasterwork in the so-called 'Chinese taste', white on a green ground. Powerscourt House, in South William Street just behind Grafton Street, was build in 1771 as the town house of Viscount Powerscourt. It has now been brought back to life as an up-market shopping and restaurant complex. Visitors have free access to the interior which has a large number of fine rooms, richly decorated with plasterwork by James McCullagh and Michael Stapleton, as well as an elaborately carved wooden staircase by Ignatius McDonagh. Probably the grandest house still in private occupation as a family residence is No 1 Grafton Street, the Provost's House, home of the Provost of Trinity College. The saloon, with its splendid, coved ceiling, runs the entire length of the building.

The north side of Dublin, originally the most fashionable sector, has suffered greatly over the years, but there are even here some remarkable pockets of survival. Henrietta Street, although sadly dilapidated, contains some of the most palatial and beautifully decorated houses in Dublin, and as a result of the dedicated work of a handful of restorationists, is undergoing a slow and painful process of recuperation. Closer to O'Connell Street is Dominick Street, where only a tiny cluster of houses remains at the top end. Luckily a number of these are quite spectacular, notably No 20, the masterwork of the stuccodore Robert West whose high relief plaster birds seem to start from the plane surfaces as if about to fly away. Between Dominick Street and O'Connell Street lies Parnell Square, now considerably defaced but retaining some very good buildings, the most notable of which are Charlemont House (now the Municipal Gallery), and the Rotunda Hospital complex, Europe's first lying-in hospital, whose chapel boasts appropriately spirited and joyful baroque plasterwork.

PLASTER DETAIL FROM DOMINICK STREET

## UNEXPECTED BEAUTIES

Parallel to Parnell Square is North Great George's Street, the sister street to Dominick Street, but unlike it almost totally intact and largely in residential ownership. An anonymous English traveller writing in 1917 in a book called *Dublin Explorations and Reflections* wrote — 'North Great George's Street, though at first glance of comparatively modest appearance, is really one of the finest streets in the whole of Dublin. Some of the empty houses, which I used to amuse myself by going over, almost took one's breath away their beauties were so unexpected.' They were built during the most brilliant period of the Ascendancy, and the interior plasterwork in the houses is by the greatest of the Irish craftsmen, Michael Stapleton, Francis Ryan and Charles Thorp among others, and ranges from rococo, with gothic covered entrance halls and trophies of birds and fruit decorating the friezes, to a more classical Adam-influenced style. Fanlights, foot scrapers and glazing bars have survived here as has an occasional lamp standard set on the railings. The elaborate doorcase of No 38, former home of Oscar Wilde's tutor Rev Sir John Pentland Mahaffy, is one of the finest in Dublin. The Loreto Convent in the middle of the street possesses one of the few remaining original Bossi fireplaces. Once a feature of great Dublin houses, these slender, elegant creations were of white marble inset with coloured stone to represent fruit, garlands or classical scenes. Crowning the street is Belvedere House, now a Jesuit College and one of the city's most splendid 18th-century mansions. The staircase here is so encrusted with plasterwork, again by Stapleton, that it has raised the fastidious disdain of some purists, but to the less severe it is an unforgettably rich and beautiful confection.

Two blocks to the east lies Mountjoy Square, of which the north and east sides are intact, the other two sides having become ruinous. However some sense of its original grandeur can be obtained by walking through the Corporation Park at its centre. A short detour into the inner suburbs will bring the traveller to a perfect and lovingly restored gem of classical architecture, the Casino at Marino, built in 1758 to the design of Sir William Chambers and now open to the public.

*BELVEDERE HOUSE · DETAIL OF PLASTERWORK*

## Literary Dublin

*W**ith her 'gentle veils of rain and all her ghosts that walk', Dublin has produced a disproportionate number of the world's great writers. Dean Swift, James Joyce, W B Yeats, Oscar Wilde and Sean O'Casey were all Dubliners, and the literary life goes on today with innovative work in the theatre.*

*BERNARD SHAW'S BIRTH PLACE*

Dublin has a long and distinguished history stretching back to medieval times, when uniquely among Irish cities Dublin had its own Mystery Play. Irish people have also always been great lovers of books as objects, as the rich decoration of the *Book of Kells* as well as the beautifully tooled book bindings of the 18th century testify, and the visitor who is interested in these things should not miss a visit to such superb collections as those held by the Library of Trinity College, Marsh's Library (close to St Patrick's Cathedral) and the Chester Beatty Library in Shrewsbury Road, which has an unparalleled display of Islamic and Oriental material. The interest in books continues today and the per capita purchase of books in the Republic is among the highest in the European community. Nevertheless an appetite to possess and decorate books is only one manifestation of interest in literature and Ireland, in particular Dublin, has produced a disproportionate number of the world's great writers. Some, like Joyce and O'Casey, have so clear a connection with the city of their birth that it is impossible to think of them as anything other than Irish. With others, however, the national identification is less clear, especially since by historical accident most of our contribution has been made in the English rather than the Irish language, and although this is fortunate in that it allows access to a much wider audience, it is somewhat galling to find figures such as Swift, Wilde and Shaw so frequently described as 'English' writers. Few nowadays recall that even Richard Steele, the great essayist who, with his friend Joseph Addison, founded and edited the *Tatler* (1709) and the *Spectator* (1711), was a Dubliner.

Two periods stand out very clearly as important ages in the history of literary Dublin — the 18th century and the early 20th century. The personality that dominates 18th-century Dublin is unquestionably that of Jonathan Swift, Dean of St Patrick's Cathedral, polemicist pamphleteer and novelist. Born in Dublin in 1667 he at first had political ambitions, but his biting tongue and gift for political satire made him too feared by the establishment for advancement, and having been made Dean of St Patrick's in 1713 he remained there for the rest of his life. He is buried near the tablet in the cathedral which bears his own Latin inscription informing the world that he has gone *ubi saeva indignatio ulterius cor lacerare nequit* — 'where savage indignation can no longer lacerate the heart'. Savage as his indignation was, he employed it in the service of humanity and his acid pen was used equally to puncture folly and pretence and to protect the defenceless. He is remembered internationally for

*Gulliver's Travels*, often thought of incorrectly as a children's book but in reality of universal appeal and application. In Dublin he is recalled also as the author of *The Drapier's Letters*, which successfully exposed and prevented the perpetration of a massive financial fraud by the government, and *A Modest Proposal*, which with bitter irony demonstrated that the children of the poor would benefit materially by being treated according to the terms of animal husbandry and fattened for the pot. With a typical mixture of black humour and humane generosity he left the bulk of his estate to found a mental hospital, St Patrick's in Dublin (still serving the community), which was unique in its time in regarding the mentally ill as patients to be comforted and treated, rather than as freaks for exhibition or exposure to teasing and ridicule, which happened in the Bethlehem (Bedlam) Hospital in London. He accompanied the benefaction with a verse in which he stated that:

> He left what little wealth he had
> To found a home for fools and mad
> And showed by one satiric touch
> No nation needed it so much.

The statue of a gentler 18th-century spirit, Oliver Goldsmith, stands in contemplation outside his old university, Trinity College. Of Goldsmith's works the stage comedy *She Stoops to Conquer* (1773), the novel *The Vicar of Wakefield* (1776) and the long narrative poem written in heroic couplet form *The Deserted Village* have survived best, bearing witness to the multiplicity of his talent. Another playwright, Richard Brinsley Sheridan, also a Trinity graduate, was born in Dublin in 1751. The house in which he was born in Dorset Street was marked with a commemorative plaque some years ago and shortly thereafter demolished. It is just as well he left behind him a monument more lasting than brass, his comedy *The Rivals* (1775) which introduced to the world the immortal Mrs Malaprop. Her resentment of 'Aspersions to my parts of speech' and statement that 'If I reprehend anything in the world it is the use of my oracular tongue and a nice derangement of epitaphs' are included in almost every dictionary of literary quotations. A third playwright of an earlier generation but again a Trinity graduate was William Congreve, one of the father figures of Restoration Drama, at least two of whose plays, *Love for Love* and *The Way of the World*, are still produced all over the world with commercial success.

**SWIFT'S SATIRE**

*I have been assured by a very knowing American of my acquaintance in London, that a young healthy child well nursed is at a year old a most delicious, nourishing, and wholesome food, whether stewed, roasted, baked, or boiled, and I make no doubt that it will equally serve in a fricassee, or a ragout.* From *A Modest Proposal*, Swift's ironic way of drawing attention to the way that poor people had to live.

*OLIVER GOLDSMITH*

## ABBEY THEATRE

Yeats's foundation of the Abbey Theatre with Lady Gregory, Edward Martyn and Annie Horniman was one of the most important events of the so-called Irish literary Renaissance. Controversy surrounded its performances from the beginning when Yeats's own play *The Countess Cathleen* was condemned as heretical by members of the Roman Catholic hierarchy. Two of the other great playwrights attracted to the Abbey by Yeats's experiments, J M Synge, born in the Dublin suburb of Rathfarnham in 1871 and Sean O'Casey, born in Dorset Street in 1884, also caused a storm with their original contributions to the theatre. Synge's first play *The Shadow* of the Glen (1903) was described in the press as 'an insult to every decent woman in Ireland', while his tragedy *Riders to the Sea* (1904) was deemed 'unfit for presentation on the stage'. The climax came with his now acclaimed comedy *The Playboy of the Western World* in January 1907. Throughout the first week the play evoked riots and a large body of police had to be deployed to quell the audience and protect the author. This was one of the not inconsiderable number of occasions in the Irish theatre on which at least as much drama occurred in the audience as on the stage. Synge died tragically early of cancer in 1909, but his plays now form part of the classical repertory of Irish drama.

Sean O'Casey, self-educated and reared in the tenement slums of the north city, was almost 40 when his first play based on 'the troubles' in Ireland was accepted by the Abbey Theatre. Just as Synge had brought the melody of Irish rural speech to the stage, so O'Casey turned his genius to recreating in the theatre the subversive wit of the Dublin poor. His second play *Juno and the Paycock* was an enormous success but the next, *The Plough and the Stars*, about the rising of Easter Week 1916 provoked an explosion similar to the *Playboy* riots, allegedly because it contained a scene in which the revolutionary flag was brought into a public house frequented by prostitutes, a class of person Dublin preferred to think it did not possess. O'Casey was bitterly disappointed when in 1928 the Abbey Board decided to reject his expressionist play about World War I, *The Silver Tassie*. He settled permanently in the south of England where he died in 1964. However, he never forgot Dublin, and the atmosphere of the city at the turn of the century as well as the quality of his own generous but quirky personality comes through clearly in the six volumes of his autobiography from *I knock at the door* to *Sunset and Evening Star*.

### JAMES JOYCE

JAMES JOYCE

Another writer who never forgot Dublin despite long absence from it was the novelist James Joyce who took the city and its inhabitants as his sole subject. Joyce was born into comfortable circumstances in suburban Dublin in 1882, but his father's bibulous incapacity for dealing with the family finances soon drove them to a life of poverty, although Joyce did somehow manage to receive an excellent education from the Jesuits at Clongowes Wood, Belvedere College and University College Dublin. Joyce was remarkably unsentimental about his native city, refusing to collaborate in its squalor by speaking of 'Dear Dirty Dublin', and labelling it the Centre of Paralysis, referring to its inhabitants as the 'most hopeless, useless and inconsistent race of characters' he had ever come across. Indeed in the posthumously published fragment *Stephen Hero* he described the brown brick houses of Dublin as representing 'the incarnation of paralysis'. His first two books *Dubliners* and *A Portrait of the Artist as a Young Man* analyse the pressures in Irish society that he felt caused this paralysis. Nevertheless he once told a friend that just as Mary felt that when she died the word 'Calais' would be found written on her heart, so after his death 'Dublin' would be found inscribed on his.

In his work there is a minute particularity of location, so that as he said himself, if Dublin were destroyed it could be rebuilt from the pages of *Ulysses*. This gigantic comic novel, published in Paris in 1922, is regarded as one of the great turning points in modern fiction, with its pioneering of the so-called 'stream of consciousness' technique. It is a multi-faceted recreation of one day, 16 June 1904, in the life of Dublin and its citizens — the day in fact upon which its author first walked out at Sandymount with the simple, elegant, Galway girl Nora Barnacle who was to become his lifelong companion. His last work, *Finnegan's Wake*, is so experimental in technique that doubts have been expressed as to whether it can be described as a novel at all. It is certainly a difficult text for the uninitiated to decipher, but listened to when read by a skilled actor it is a unique distillation of the essence of the city he both loved and hated. Many other prose writers, notably George Moore, Oliver Gogarty, Flann O'Brien, James Plunkett, J P Donleavy, Lee Dunne, Val Mulkerns and Maeve Binchy, have written hauntingly and humorously about Dublin, but none has given its image so definitively to the world as Joyce. The Martello Tower at Sandycove, setting of the opening scene of *Ulysses*, has been made into a James Joyce Museum in his honour.

## ULSTER POETS

Of course not all those who have written about Dublin have been Dubliners themselves. The Ulster poet Louis McNeice writes movingly about Dublin:

> With her seedy elegance
> With her gentle veils of rain
> And all her ghosts that walk
> And all that hide behind
> Her Georgian façades.

His fellow poet from Monaghan, Patrick Kavanagh, said that the worst mistake he ever made was coming to Dublin but he nevertheless celebrated in his verse the inner suburbs of the city. One of his lyrics, *Raglan Road*, recalls a chance encounter on a suburban street, the words fitted to an old Irish air 'the Dawning of the Day'.

An institution of the Dublin literary scene to which Kavanagh was much attached was the literary pub, such as McDaid's in Harry Street, the Bailey and Davy Byrne's in Duke Street and the Palace Bar in Fleet Street. Many of these, however, have come to the notice of the tourist — through novels or volumes of reminiscences by writers such as Anthony Cronin or John Ryan — and the whims of the publicity-shy literati have carried them off elsewhere. However, in most Dublin pubs you are likely to find the raw material of talk upon which so many writers drew.

## MOORE'S MELODIES

In 19th-century Dublin, poetry predominated with figures such as Thomas Moore who staked his reputation on the enormously long *Lalla Rookh* which is now almost forgotten, although his *Irish Melodies*, poems such as *The Last Rose of Summer* and *She is far from the land*, written to fit the rhythmic pattern of traditional Irish airs, remain popular items in the concert repertoire of tenor singers. In

**PATRICK KAVANAGH**

*On Raglan Road on an autumn day I met her first and knew That her dark hair would weave a snare that I might one day rue.*

*Ulysses* James Joyce, who disliked the sentimentality of many of the 'melodies', has his character Leopold Bloom reflect on glancing at the statue of the poet in College Green that they did right to install the image of the author of 'The Meeting of the Waters' on top of a gents' urinal. The statue is still there, but the subterranean loo is closed, its roof used as a base for rainfall-measuring instruments. A less fortunate poet was James Clarence Mangan who specialised in translations from Irish and continental languages and indeed even from languages he did not understand, or had invented himself. Mangan, who died in 1849, is the author or translator of the patriotic poem *Dark Rosaleen*. Addicted to opium and alcohol he had a miserable life seeking refuge from the world among the venerable tomes of the Trinity College Library where he held a lowly clerkship. Happier in life was the Northerner Sir Samuel Ferguson, one of the early cultural nationalists who for many years held a brilliant salon at his residence No 20 North Great George's Street. In the field of drama Ireland's main contribution was probably made by Dion Boucicault, born in 1820 in a house in Gardiner Street which is now demolished. Renowned for the creation of melodramas such as *The Colleen Bawn* and *Conn the Shaughraun*, with his mastery of theatrical effect he influenced not only Irish dramatists like Sean O'Casey and Brendan Behan, both born within a stone's throw of Gardiner Street themselves, but also, through his tours of the US, American playwrights like Tennessee Williams and Eugene O'Neill.

### W B YEATS

*And I shall have some peace there, for peace comes dropping slow,*
*Dropping from the veils of the morning to where the cricket sings;*
*There midnight's all a-glimmer, and noon a purple glow,*
*And evening full of the linnet's wings.*

*Lake Isle of Innisfree,*
W B Yeats

### YEATS AND WILDE

The second half of the 19th century saw the birth in the Dublin suburb of Sandymount, in 1867, of one of the world's greatest poets, the Nobel prizewinner William Butler Yeats. The Yeats family were from Sligo, and Yeats, although he was educated at the High School, Dublin (then in Harcourt Street) and spent a good deal of his young manhood in London, hankered for the west of Ireland. This spirit infuses much of his melodic early poetry such as *The Lake Isle of Innisfree, Down by the Salley Gardens* and *The Stolen Child*. The progenitor of the Celtic Twilight and the Abbey Theatre, he was made a Senator of the newly formed Free State, serving from 1922 to 1928, and his home on the west side of Merrion Square carries a commemorative plaque.

Across the Square at No 1 lived Sir William and Lady Wilde, the parents of Oscar Wilde, who was born around the corner in Westland Row in 1856. Sir William was a distinguished eye surgeon and antiquarian, and, in marked contrast to his eldest son, a determined womaniser, a fact which does not seem to have greatly troubled his wife who concentrated on writing a great volume of nationalistic verse under the pen name of Speranza. Oscar Wilde was one of the most brilliant undergraduates in the Trinity of his day, but soon made his way to Oxford where he won the Newdigate Prize and made a reputation for the eccentricity of his dress and the scintillating wit of his conversation. His own view of the Irish was that we are 'a nation of brilliant failures, but the greatest talkers since the Greeks'. Indeed the term Wildean has become an accolade of brilliance in conversation. His first successful work was a novel, *The Picture of Dorian Gray*, a stylised *roman-à-clef* full of symbolic references to his homosexual inclinations that were subsequently turned against him at his notorious trials in London. George Bernard Shaw (also Dublin born) was among those who defended him. Wilde was a master of epigram and of paradox ('work is the curse of the drinking classes', says one of his characters) and he took London by storm producing four superb comedies in quick succession — *Lady Windermere's Fan* in 1892, *A Woman of No Importance* in 1893, *An Ideal Husband* and *The Importance of Being Earnest* in 1895.

## THEATRE TODAY

It should not be felt that Dublin's literary life is all in the past. In the fifties and sixties there was a significant revival in the theatre with the presentation of original works by a new generation of Irish playwrights — Samuel Beckett, Brendan Behan and Hugh Leonard — and an international theatre festival of some distinction was established. This takes place annually in October and up to 50 plays from all over the world are performed in a three-week period. The Theatre Festival has an office in Nassau Street. Of the theatres themselves, the Abbey Theatre, rebuilt on its original site in Abbey Street after a disastrous fire in 1951, has become a national institution, while the Gaiety Theatre in North King Street, at the top of Grafton Street, and the Olympia Theatre in Dame Street have been recently refurbished. One delightful smaller theatre is the Gate Theatre in the Rotunda Complex at the top of O'Connell Street. The Gate developed an international reputation under the guidance of its reigning partnership of Micheal MacLiammoir and Hilton Edwards for nearly 40 years from the early 1930s, training actors like Orson Welles who went on to international stardom. After they had both died in the 1970s fears were expressed for its survival, but in recent years a new eminently successful and innovative management under the direction of Michael Colgan has made it one of the most exciting and popular theatrical venues in the city. The Tivoli is a large, recently opened theatre in Francis Street. A popular theatrical venue is the new Andrew's Lane Theatre and studio, where a wide variety of productions includes a special interest in new Irish writing. At the Project Theatre in East Essex Street, interesting work has been carried out by the playwright Peter Sheridan and his director/ producer brother Jim Sheridan, best known for his work on the film *My Left Foot*. Deirdre O'Connell's experience of the Stanislavsky Studio in New York has influenced productions of Ibsen and Strindberg among others at the Focus Theatre behind Leeson Street. Vigorous peripatetic theatrical companies include Roddy Doyle's Passion Machine, which has succeeded in bringing Irish plays to a new audience, as well as the Rough Magic, Smock Alley, the Pig's Back and Co-motion companies.

The Dublin Writers Museum in Parnell Square traces the relationship of writers with the city, and wherever you walk in Dublin you can be sure that you are close to some aspect of literary history.

*OSCAR WILDE*

# Traditional Music

*I*ntricate variations on an age-old tune, 'battering' out the steps of a country dance, sing-along sessions at the pub, feasts of music for musicians from round the world . . . all these are aspects of traditional Irish music, which began in farmhouse kitchens and now enjoys new life as an essential part of the city scene.*

One of the most attractive features of Dublin night life — for visitor and native alike — is the number of music and singing pubs which flourish both in the city centre and suburbs. The music provided in these establishments varies from sing-along with piano accompaniment to organised groups in ballad sessions or informal sessions of instrumental traditional music to which the listeners may from time to time dance Irish country-dances or 'sets'.

### CÉILÍ NIGHTS

At the turn of the century, Irish traditional music was the popular music favoured by the vast majority of the Irish people. In the countryside and in the numerous small towns and villages, it was the music played when people assembled in someone's home, at crossroads or in village halls, for a 'night', 'scoraíocht', or 'soirée'. The most basic and frequent of these events was the session at the céilí-house — or scoraíochting-house — there being some such house in every townland. It might be any house in the area that was suitably situated, and where the good man and woman of the house liked music and company and didn't make too much fuss about getting to bed at an early hour. Preferably it would have a spacious kitchen with a stone-flagged floor.

At these houses the young men and girls, as well as some of the older folk from a radius of half a mile or so, would assemble on a couple of nights a week. There might be as many as twenty-five or thirty people involved, or as few as seven or eight. They whiled away the hours between milking time and bedtime — both conveniently variable — with talking, card-playing, story-telling or dancing.

Sets or half-sets would be the order of the night — traditional group dances, usually danced by four couples. There are numerous regional kinds and variations. In some parts of the country, however, the Lancers, the barn-dance and even the waltz were not unknown. The music would be provided on a fiddle or concertina, or if need be one of the company would lilt the required tunes.

Dancers who prided themselves on their footwork vied with one another in 'battering' out intricate rhythms on the stout flags of the farmhouse kitchen floor. (Battering in this context refers to the dancers' lively footwork.) There might be a few songs, usually comic songs or songs about some local incident. In areas where there was a strong singing tradition, there might be a particular house or night for singing rather than dancing, but music and dancing were the rule.

These nights of music-making took place all the year round, though in many areas they were either abandoned or operated at a low key during Lent. There were also 'special nights', such as balls, weddings and threshing nights. These were attended by large numbers of people so that not only the house but also the barn or some such spacious outhouse would be used. It was common practice throughout most of the country that all musicians who were willing to play had an open invitation to such functions. So it was that the musician was frequently to be seen heading homewards to the song of the lark in the morning.

Travelling musicians who sang and played at markets and fairs helped to bring tunes and songs from one area to another. Travelling and local musicians were also willing, for a few pence per lesson — or sometimes, in the case of the former, for their keep — to pass on their skills and tunes to aspiring youngsters.

Such then, was the standing and place of Irish traditional music in the lives of the people in the greater part of rural Ireland about the turn of the century. The cities, such as Dublin, Cork, Galway and Belfast, also had traditional music communities where immigrants from the provinces compared and swapped tunes with the native traditional musicians.

## DECLINE AND REVIVAL

The 1930s and 1940s were poor times in Ireland, and emigration seemed set to drain perpetually the life blood of youth from her shores. At this time Irish music was flourishing and popular amongst the Irish emigrants in the cities of England and the USA. Michael Coleman, the most celebrated of all Irish traditional fiddlers, recorded more than 60 records in New York in the 1920s and 1930s. But at home, the Dance Halls Act was opening the way for commercial dance halls where modern dance bands were introducing the foxtrot, the tango and the hokey cokey in an atmosphere far removed from the house-dance scene. Young people were flocking in thousands to these 'Ballrooms of Romance' and, for a period at least, the era of the céilí-house-dance was at an end. The morale among musicians was at a low ebb and attitudes to the music were unenlightened, even derisory.

Since music in the pubs had not been the practice up to this time, there were very few places where the traditional musician could find an appreciative audience. Many were inclined to put away the fiddles and the flutes entirely, but a determined core of musicians, who met regularly at the Pipers' Club at 14 Thomas Street in the Dublin Liberties, decided that they would organise an annual nationwide gathering of musicians. Having made contact with fellow enthusiasts in other parts of the country, they planned the first Fleadh Cheoil (literally a 'feast of music') which took place in Mullingar in May 1951. It was successful enough to warrant another try, and so was born the traditional music organisation Comhaltas Ceoltóirí Éireann (literally Fellowship of Musicians of Ireland) and the Fleadhanna Cheoil.

### GLOSSARY

**sets** traditional group dances usually danced by four couples.

**scoraíochting-house** or **céilí house** a house where people gather for a social evening.

**battering** the lively footwork of a skilled set-dancer.

**Comhaltas Ceoltóirí Eireann** Fellowship of Muscians of Ireland.

**Fleadh Cheoil** feast of music.

**céilí band** group of musicians who play traditional music.

### FIRST FLEADHANNA

Those first Fleadhanna Cheoil (literally 'feasts of music') gave traditional musicians a platform where they could play to a really appreciative audience and where traditional style was the rule. The sun always seemed to shine at those early Fleadhanna too, as men and women took down fiddles and flutes that had lain idle for years and hit the road for Cavan and Loughrea with lightness in their step and a tune in their hearts.

While the primary purpose of the Fleadhanna Cheoil was (and continues to be) the holding of competitions on various instruments, many musicians came just for the sheer enjoyment of playing music and meeting musicians arriving from other areas. Informal sessions of music, in pubs and on the streets, would go on all day and into the early hours, and although the Fleadh officially concluded on Monday evening, the music and revelry would last well into midweek. Within the space of a few years the mood of the Irish music would have swung from depression to an all time 'high'.

Through the 1950s the Fleadh and Comhaltas grew hand in hand. Irish exiles soon began to take an active part and musicians living in Liverpool, Birmingham, London and New York began coming over to the Fleadh, and so another dimension was added. Branches of Comhaltas sprang up all over Ireland, organising classes, concerts and sessions at local level. With a countrywide network of activity established from the mid-1950s or so, traditional music was already riding high by the time of the international ballad boom in the early 1960s.

The situation was further consolidated through a massive teaching campaign which commenced in the mid-1960s and through which numerous fiddlers, flute players, pipers and other musicians were encouraged to pass on their music and music styles to the younger generation. The results of this network of classes can be seen in the huge numbers of younger people now playing the old music in the old style.

### INSTRUMENTS

Of the instruments normally used in playing Irish traditional music the only uniquely Irish instrument is the **uilleann pipes**, so called because these sweet-sounding pipes are blown by a bellows under the arm and elbow (*uilleann* is the Gaelic for elbow). The **fiddle**, the **two-row accordion**, the **wooden concert flute**, the **tin whistle** and the **banjo** are very popular. The **concertina**, **piano accordion** and **mandolin** are less widely played, except for Co Clare where the concertina has for many years been very much in favour, especially with lady musicians. The **harp** has seen a revival in recent years. The **guitar**, the **bouzouki** and the **piano** are the instruments mostly used for accompaniment. The **bodhran**, a simple hand-held goatskin drum, is widely used, and rhythms may be tapped out with a pair of **bones** or **spoons**. **Drums** are usual in céilí bands.

### THE PLAYER'S ART

Irish traditional music comes in two forms — vocal and instrumental. The latter is mostly dance music — reels, jigs, hornpipes, polkas, set-dances, mazurkas — the remainder being marches, slow airs (usually song tunes) and 'planxties' (harpers' pieces which have survived from the 17th or 18th centuries). These tunes have various origins, but it is possible to state generally that they were mostly composed in the 18th and 19th centuries, that they were passed down aurally through generations of music makers and that practitioners of the art of traditional music share a common approach and set of techniques in their interpretation of this music. Within this common approach there are standards — accepted by performers and enlightened listeners — by which one judges a musician's ability to interpret, rework and refurbish the old tunes, through the use of various forms of ornamentation and of melodic and rhythmic variation. These variations and ornamentations are generally minor ones, involving just a few notes in a particular phase of a tune, yet when executed with skill and subtlety they can show a considerable level of imagination and even creativity. One is more likely to find this kind of music where music is played for listening, rather than where the dance tunes are 'belted out' for a set, but even in the latter case the musician will usually try to give the tunes that little bit extra in rhythm (called 'lift' or 'swing' in traditional music) which will add zest to the dancing.

## OLD SONGS, NEW STYLES

Traditional songs in Ireland include the old songs in Irish which may be heard in the Gaeltacht (Irish-speaking) areas along the western coast, and which are sung in what is called the 'sean nós' or 'old style'; and songs in the English language (but with an Irish character or flavour) of which there are numerous examples in various regional and personal styles.

Solo unaccompanied singing is the usual means of presentation and many traditional songs may run to eight or ten minutes, which tends to limit the appeal of traditional singing to a small circle of devotees. The best songs and singing styles demand a high degree of vocal artistry and interpretation and several of the finest traditional singers — such as Paddy Tunney and the late Seosamh Ó hÉanai — have won international recognition. But these serious demanding songs with their intricate melodies and niceties of embellishment are not the ideal stuff for the noisy atmosphere of a pub session. A lighter, more boisterous type of song with a bit of backing is more appropriate to such a situation. With the great international 'ballad boom' of the 1960s, groups singing the lighter or simpler ballads, to guitar accompaniment, found a ready market in clubs and pubs throughout Ireland. The McPeakes of Belfast, and the Clancy Brothers and Tommy Makem were first in the field; and the Dubliners and the Wolfe Tones have been among the most successful of these groups. The old styles of solo singing still flourish, however, and may be heard at special traditional singing sessions such as the Fleadh in Ballycastle, Co Antrim, at An t-Oireachtas (the great annual Irish language festival), at the Cultúrlann, Monkstown, Co Dublin or at Fleadh Cheoil na hÉireann.

Traditional singers such as Len Graham, Kevin Cuniffe and Dolores Keane also help to introduce the old songs to a wider audience, by singing the occasional solo in traditional style, during a performance with a group.

## WHERE TO HEAR IT

Traditional music, singing and dancing can be found at pubs and other venues in Dublin all year round. A list of these is given in the Directory, page 83.

Sessions are held at the Cultúrlann, 32 Belgrave Square, Monkstown, Co Dublin (easily reached by DART trains from the city centre) on Fridays and Saturdays all year round, and from Monday to Saturday from June to early September. This is the headquarters of Comhaltas Ceoltóirí Éireann.

Out of the city, the best areas for music in the pubs are Clare, Galway and South Sligo, but sessions will be found in most other areas too. Details in local papers.

Fleadhanna Cheoil are held at County and Provincial level throughout the country from May to August, culminating in the 'All Ireland' Fleadh Cheoil na hÉireann, in a different place each year.

# Gardens of Dublin County

*T*hink of Ireland and you think of lush green
gardens and parks and a landscape of true
natural beauty. The gentle climate which makes
Ireland so green favours horticulture, and in
Dublin's gardens can be seen many tender and
exotic plants.

William Butler Yeats wrote of those 'gardens where a
soul's at ease', and within short distances of the centre of
this busy city weary travellers will find such tranquil
gardens, flower-filled and enhanced with emerald green
lawns. Each has its own character, its own setting, and
above all its own charm.

What makes an Irish garden special? The mild, moist
climate is a major contributing factor. Mildness is a
relative matter, but Ireland does not suffer from the
excesses of frost and snow, or sun and drought, that can
hamper gardeners in some other lands. Ireland's gardeners
do complain too often about the rain, but that very rain
helps to keep their lawns green through the summer, and
provides the moisture to enable the cultivation of some
most exotic plants. But the more ordinary plants flourish
too, and the visitor can discover the very finest spring
bulbs and roses, many of them raised here by world-
famous breeders.

The Dublin area is not the mildest part of Ireland, but
the coastal fringe enjoys an enviable climate for
gardening. Frost is infrequent within sight of the sea, and
as long as there is shelter from the east winds of winter,
exotic plants from all over the world will flourish. So
within the region about Dublin it is possible to see some
of those rare plants for which Irish gardens are famous —
tree-ferns from Tasmania, rhododendrons from western
China, and the blue crocus from Chile.

Landscape and soil also have significant effects upon
gardens. About Dublin, especially to the south, an acid
soil prevails and this enables gardeners to cultivate
camellias and rhododendrons with consummate ease. But
the heavy clays of the counties lying west of the city are
not barren; these places do have harsher winters, but fine
aboreta — at Birr Castle, for example — with
incomparable collections of rare trees have been
established there, and should not be overlooked by keen
gardeners.

BOTANICAL GARDENS LAKE

DEER IN PHOENIX PARK

## FORMAL GARDENS

Undoubtedly the finest use of the landscape is seen at
Powerscourt, where a superb formal garden, rising terrace
by terrace from a small lake, is overshadowed by the
Dublin Mountains. The Sugarloaf dominates the skyline,
and is an integral part of the whole grand design.
Nineteenth-century Powerscourt is one of the best
examples of formal gardening in Ireland. Close by is
Kilruddery, which predates Powerscourt by a century and
more. The Sugarloaf is still visible in Kilruddery but it does
not form a focal point. Instead, two parallel canals, in the
French manner, lead from the house into a ride; beside
them are The Angles, formal hedges of hornbeam and
beech.

On an altogether grander scale is Phoenix Park; with an
area of 1752 acres, it is the largest enclosed park in any
European city. Its magnificent central avenue — sadly
now a busy thoroughfare — is lined with beautiful trees.
On crisp winter mornings when the sun shines weakly, or
on warm summer afternoons, 'the Park' is a quiet haven.
A herd of deer roams freely, and nestling in one
sequestered corner are the Zoological Gardens, surely the
prettiest zoo in Europe.

Formality prevails in the city's smaller parks. At St
Anne's in Clontarf, summer beds of beautiful roses delight
the eye and the nose. St Stephen's Green, in the heart of
the city, and Merrion Square deserve the visitor's
attention, and so does the lawned oasis of Trinity College,
wherein gardens have been carefully tended for four
centuries; the newest of the College squares was laid out
under the supervision of Lanning Roper.

One of the best-known gardens within the city limits is
the Islandbridge National War Memorial, a *tour de force* of
stone and formal planting which is one of the
achievements of Sir Edwin Lutyens, the great English
architect. Sadly neglected for many years, it is now being
restored. Lutyens also restyled 14th-century Howth Castle
on Dublin Bay, noted for its wild rhododendron garden
begun little more than a century ago.

## WILD GARDENS

The Irish character does not easily slip into imposed order,
and since the mid-1800s, Irish gardeners have shied away

from rigid lines. Indeed the principles of the wild garden, in which plants have free rein to grow and multiply, were promoted by an Irishman, William Robinson. His ideas can best be appreciated in the celebrated Mount Usher Garden to the south of Dublin in Co Wicklow where a bubbling river is wrapped in a cloak of tall gum-trees. There is a stunning Mexican pine, colourful rhododendrons and a host of other exotic plants, too tender to survive out-of-doors except in the balmy, moist atmosphere of this sheltered valley. Here the plants grow naturally, the lawns are trimmed only when the flowering bulbs have set their seeds, and weedkillers are never used. And this is where that blue crocus blooms.

There is much to delight the visitor in the smaller Dublin gardens. Fernhill and the Talbot Gardens at Malahide contain collections of rare trees and shrubs, ranging from the magnolias of the Himalayas to flame-trees of Chile, from the white-blossomed tree poppy of California to the daisy-bushes of New Zealand. Spring bulbs and the russet leaves of autumn make these, and other gardens, places for all seasons.

Of the two botanical gardens, the smaller one, only two decades old but with roots going back three hundred years and more, is maintained by Trinity College, Dublin. Both native and exotic plants are grown principally for teaching purposes, and the botanists of the University recently mounted a rescue mission to save some of the endangered plants of Mauritius.

Only two centuries have elapsed since the National Botanic Gardens were founded at Glasnevin, a short journey from central Dublin, but it is Ireland's premier garden and one of the world's greatest botanical gardens. Within there is an ancient yew walk probably planted in the 1740s, and the magnificent cast-iron glasshouse erected and designed by Richard Turner in the mid-1800s, sister to the Great Palm House of Kew Gardens in London. Tens of thousands of different plants — orchids, palms, giant water lilies, dove trees, and the native Killarney fern — are displayed in these 50 magnificent acres.

Whether the garden is large or small, formal or wild, linger a while and seek the quietude that comes with shady trees, green grass and scented flowers. About Dublin you can, with ease, find W B Yeat's 'bee-loud glade' not far from the city in beautiful Irish gardens.

MOUNT USHER GARDENS

# PLACES TO VISIT

Museums, galleries, famous buildings, public
gardens, walking tours

### Abbey Presbyterian Church

*Parnell Square*

A prominent landmark with its white neo-Gothic clocktower and slender spire, the church has many fine stone carvings, over the doorway and at the bases of window arches. It was completed in 1864 and the building cost of £20,000 was met by Alex Findlater, a Scot who established a leading grocery chain and brewery in Dublin; it is widely known as Findlater's Church. The church overlooks the Garden of Remembrance which commemorates those who gave their lives for Irish freedom. The Children of Lir sculpture at the west end, by Oisin Kelly, recalls a legend of children being turned into swans.

### Abbey Theatre

*Marlborough Street*

This stark modern block, designed by Michael Scott, replaces a smaller Abbey which opened in 1904 in a building which had been a music hall and a morgue, and which was bought and equipped as a theatre by Annie Horniman. W B Yeats, Edward Martyn and Augusta Lady Gregory were the young Abbey's moving spirits and John Millington Synge its first controversial playwright. His *Playboy of the Western World* caused rioting in the theatre in 1907 among a sensitively nationalistic audience who were not prepared for its realism.

BANK OF IRELAND

There was further rioting in the Abbey in 1926 when Sean O'Casey's *The Plough and the Stars* was first staged here. Many of the audience regarded it as a cynical view of the 1916 Rebellion. The Abbey Players achieved an international reputation but in the 1940s, with Yeats dead, it was felt that the Abbey had lost the motivation necessary to its status as a national theatre. However, a plan put forward to demolish it and build a three-part national theatre on the site was shelved after a change of Government. On 17 July 1951 the Abbey was destroyed by fire. The present Abbey and Peacock complex opened exactly 15 years later.

### Aldborough House

*Portland Row*

A brick mansion with a granite façade, this was the last great town house of the 18th century, and was completed in 1796 for Edward Stratford, Earl of Aldborough, by William Chambers. Some of its original ornamentation in Portland stone was badly corroded by the salty air of the Bay, which then lay much closer to the house than now. In 1813 it became the Feinaglin Institute, a school using a revolutionary system of memory training. Later a barrack, and now accommodating Post Office staff, the house retains its fine interior. It overlooks the Five Lamps, a monument to Galway-born General Henry Hall of the Indian army. It is not open to the public.

### Bank of Ireland

*College Green*

Formerly the Irish Parliament House, this striking windowless edifice has 22 pillars in its grand portico, which is 147ft long. Over its pediment are figures of Hibernia, Commerce and Fidelity, and those of Fortitude, Justice and Liberty can be seen over another portico in Westmorland Street. The main architect was Edward Lovett Pearce, and the building took from 1729 to 1739 to erect. There were later additions by James Gandon and Francis Johnston.

The former House of Commons is now the Banking Mall and may be seen during banking hours. In the House of Lords, with its coffered ceiling, fine oak woodwork and large tapestries, is the mace of the old

Commons speaker. On Tuesdays, guided tours are available, and occasionally the House of Lords is an attractive venue for concerts.

The Act of Union of 1800 ended the building's days as a parliament house. Its most famous parliamentarian had been Henry Grattan, whose statue by John Henry Foley is in the roadway opposite. The nearby Thomas Davis statue is by Edward Delaney.

### Belvedere House

*Great Denmark Street*

Begun in 1775 for George Rochford, Lord Belvedere, this mansion contains some of the finest plasterwork of the celebrated Michael Stapleton, including the Apollo, Diana and Venus rooms, though the Venus ceiling's centrepiece was removed when the building became a boys' college in 1841. There are fireplaces by Bossi, the Venetian master, and bronze Apollo medallions on the staircase handrails.

George Rochford died in 1814 and the house, commanding one of the finest urban views of the day down the Georgian North Great George's Street, was sold to the Jesuits 27 years later for use as a college. It is a famous rugby school, and its most celebrated pupil was undoubtedly James Joyce, who lived nearby. (He was born south of the city at 41 Brighton Square, Rathgar.)

### Bewley's Cafés

*Grafton Street and elsewhere*

Bewley's Oriental Cafés have been a Dublin tradition for well over a century, and the Bewleys have been one of the city's best-known Quaker families. They began as tea and coffee merchants in Sycamore Street some time before 1842, and the idea of opening cafés sprang from the insistence of customers on sampling the products before purchase. The retail side of the business continues.

The cafés are in Grafton Street, South Great George's Street and Westmoreland Street, with smaller outlets elsewhere. They are noted for their old-world atmosphere and appearance. Particularly striking are the façades in Grafton Street — where mahogany and mosaics are oddly juxtaposed — and Westmoreland Street, recently but imaginatively rebuilt after a fire.

Bewley's emerged under new management from a financial crisis in 1986. The cafés and shops, however, retain most of their traditional charm. The Grafton Street café has a small museum.

### Bluecoat School

*Blackhall Place*

The school, now occupied by the Incorporated Law Society, is a splendid Palladian building by Thomas Ivory, built in 1773-83; the cupola was added in 1904. The boardroom is noted for a fine plaster ceiling (1778-80) by Charles Thorp, though some of it is later, repair work.

The school was founded in 1669 and moved to a site outside the city in 1970. It was variously called the Bluecoat School, King's Hospital School and Bluecoat Boys' Hospital, but its formal title was Hospital and Free School of King Charles II. Its uniform of a navy blue cutaway brass-buttoned coat with navy blue knee breeches, yellow waistcoats, long yellow stockings and silver shoe buckles was only discarded for something less flamboyant in 1923. The choirboys still wear scarlet cassocks.

The ground at the back of the building, formerly a playing field, is the last surviving part of Oxmantown Green, once the central feature of a large Viking settlement.

### Botanic Gardens

*See National Botanic Gardens (page 47).*

### Brazen Head

*Lower Bridge Street*

This four-storey hostelry with its sunken courtyard is Dublin's oldest inn. It was constructed in about 1666, but seems to have been built on the site of a much older establishment, and its foundations certainly predate the 17th century. Visitors will notice that it is built at a lower level than its surroundings.

In James Joyce's *Ulysses*, Stephen Dedalus is told that 'you get a decent enough do in the Brazen Head over in Winetavern Street for a bob', a rare example of the expatriate Joyce, writing from memory, placing something in the wrong street.

Irish patriots Robert Emmet, Wolfe Tone, Henry Grattan, Daniel O'Connell and William Smith O'Brien were all patrons of the Brazen Head. The revolutionary United Irishmen regularly met in it, and some of their leaders were arrested here in 1797. A desk used by Emmet, who stayed in the inn, stood for many years in a corner of the bar, but was later moved to an upstairs room.

### Casino, Marino

*Malahide Road*

The Casino stands in what was part of the grounds of the now-demolished Marino House. It was built in 1758 from a plan by Sir William Chambers and has been called one of the world's most perfect Palladian buildings. The original furniture has long gone but the structure was extensively restored by the Office of Public Works in the early 1980s and may be visited daily in summer.

Surrounded by twelve Tuscan columns, eight in the four porticoes and four at the corners, it is based on Palladio's idea of the symmetrical villa and incorporates his notion of a temple façade running all around a building. Lions guard the approaches, and the graceful urns adorning the roof are outlets for a central heating system in the walls, operated by lighting fires in the grates. The building's ornate fireplaces and the jasper inlays in its doorstep indicate the opulence Lord Charlemont had in mind when he had it built as a 'pleasure-house', and wine cellars running off the surrounding basement area hint at convivial evenings. Balustrades, pediments and festooned panels hide the top storey; and the free-standing columns and urns stress the mathematical precision.

Marino Crescent, at the bottom of Malahide Road, was built in 1792 by a painter named ffolliott, enemy of Lord Charlemont, to block the sea view from Marino House. Bram Stoker, author of *Dracula*, was born at No 15 in 1847.

### Chester Beatty Library and Gallery of Oriental Art

*20 Shrewsbury Road*

This contains the collection of Sir Alfred Chester Beatty, mining engineer and philanthropist, and comprises not only an outstanding assembly of books, including many 14th- and 15th-century French volumes, but a large number of paintings, papyri, bindings, wall hangings, costumes, carvings, drawings, Babylonian clay tablets and other artefacts illustrating the history of humanity from 2700BC to the present. The collection of Islamic material is particularly fine, and the huge array of Japanese prints, including hundreds of *surimono*, is one of the best of its kind.

Opened to the public in 1954, the library and gallery can be visited all day Tuesday to Friday, and on Saturday afternoons.

The building's central section was erected around the ceiling of the Chinese Room, which is made up of 200 panels from an ancient temple. The Garden Room, with its illuminated Persian manuscripts and Armenian Gospels, was a favourite haunt of Chester Beatty himself in his declining years. He had never been able to survey his collection properly before its display here, and even now the full collection cannot be shown all at once.

### Christ Church Cathedral

*Christ Church Place*

Christ Church, whose official name is the Cathedral of the Holy Trinity, replaced a timber church founded on the same site in 1038 by the Viking King Sitric. The cathedral is related in style to Glastonbury and Wells, and is, with St Patrick's, one of the best examples in Ireland of early Gothic architecture. Its large groin-vaulted crypt, crossing and transepts are its oldest parts, the crypt dating from 1172. Lambert Simnel, the Boy Pretender, was 'crowned' as King Edward VI of England here in 1487, using a crown borrowed from a statue of the Virgin Mary, possibly one which still exists in the Carmelite church in Whitefriar Street. In 1539 Archbishop Browne, flushed with the zeal of the Reformation, publicly burned relics here, which were said to include the staff of St Patrick, brought from Armagh; in 1559 a parliament was held in the cathedral and about 20 years later the nave had become a bazaar and there were taverns in the crypt.

Christ Church fell into such disrepair that its 1871–78 restoration involved considerable rebuilding. This was financed by distiller Henry Roe, and the architect was G E Street.

### The nave

The interior of the Cathedral is extremely beautiful, an outstanding feature being the magnificent stonework of the nave and aisles. The nave was begun in 1213, its most westerly bay, different from the others, being built around 1234. It contains three prominent sarcophagi. One is that of a Bishop Lindsay who died in 1846, on whose land in Glasnevin the Holy Faith convent and schools were built. But controversy surrounds the two facing it across the church: the effigy of a recumbent knight with a smaller figure lying beside him. Some people maintain that they contain the remains of Strongbow, Anglo-Norman coloniser, and his son, whom he is said to have killed for fleeing from a battle. Others believe that they are the tombs of Strongbow and his consort Eva, while a third opinion insists that they have nothing to do with Strongbow at all. Strongbow, Earl of Pembroke, died in Dublin in 1177 and one school of thought maintains that his tomb, while certainly in this cathedral, cannot be identified since being damaged in a roof fall in 1562.

### The choir

The present choir dates from Street's restoration of the 1870s and resembles the pre-1350 one which he believed to be the original. None the less he was attacked for 'destroying a 14th-century choir of unique interest', which Sir Richard Colt Hoare had called 'an unnatural medley of Gothic and Italian architecture'.

### Exterior

In the grounds on the south side are ruins of the chapterhouse of an Augustinian priory which was attached to the cathedral until the Reformation. The arch of the cathedral's great south door is typically late 12th-century Norman. The Synod House, which dates from the 1871 restoration, is being developed as a Medieval Heritage Centre. The tower is a remnant of the demolished medieval St Michael's Church. The tower on Christ Church itself is a 1330 construction. The cathedral's south wall was rebuilt by Street, who also added the flying buttresses on the north side.

## City Hall

*Lord Edward Street*

The first Earl of Cork had a mansion on this site, and later the Church of St Mary del Dame and a city gate called Dame's Gate stood here. The City Hall, with its fine six-columned Corinthian portico, closes the view up Parliament Street from the Liffey. This was the first street laid out by the Wide Streets Commission in the 18th century, when the bridge at its foot was the lowest on the river and the route from the north side to the parliament house led through it.

Thomas Cooley designed the City Hall (1769-79) as the Royal Exchange, and Thomas Ivory's 1781 municipal buildings above it were originally a bank. Inside the hall's balustrade, with its urns and four black trefoils of lamps, is an empty plinth. It was meant for a statue of Daniel O'Connell, who included a spell as Lord Mayor of Dublin among his achievements. The statue, by John Hogan, is inside the building, as are marble statues of Thomas Davis, Dr Charles Lucas and Thomas Drummond, the latter also by Hogan. Lucas was an 18th-century apothecary in the city who advocated the reform of the Corporation and opposed attempts by the English parliament to impose its will on Ireland. He was praised as a pioneer of Irish liberty by Henry Grattan; his statue is by Edward Smyth. Drummond was an organiser of the Royal Irish Constabulary. A fine marble statue of Henry Grattan by Sir Francis Chantrey is in a stairwell on the right.

The building's beautiful coffered dome is best viewed from inside the circular central hall.

## Civic Museum

*See Dublin Civic Museum (page 39).*

## Custom House

*Custom House Quay*

One of Ireland's finest buildings, the

Custom House is usually viewed from across the Liffey, and much of its exquisite detail is missed. It is 375ft long and 205ft deep, and its sides almost exactly face the principal compass points. The central front projection is joined to the end pavilions by arcades, each with seven arches, and all the columns along the building's front have harps in the capitals. The graceful copper dome, with its four pedimented clocks, brings the height to 120ft, and above this rises a 16ft figure of Hope, resting on her anchor.

Below the building's dividing frieze, 13 heads of riverine gods represent 13 Irish rivers. These form the keystones of arches. Over the main door a 14th head is a female representation of the Atlantic Ocean. Several bovine heads recall the port's beef trade. The four statues along the back of the building represent Europe, Asia, Africa and America. The building's back and side are of mountain granite, the front of Portland stone.

The building of the Custom House (1781-91) was opposed by local residents who feared that it would make the area a slum, by commercial interests from an older custom house upriver and by the Dublin Corporation. Hired mobs pulled up piles and architect James Gandon often appeared on the site wearing his sword.

During fighting in 1921 the Custom House was burned to a shell, but it was rebuilt with all the glory of the original.

## Dublin Castle

### Cork Hill

King John ordered the building of Dublin Castle in 1204 as part of the city's defensive system. It was threatened by Edward de Bruce in 1317, besieged by Silken Thomas Fitzgerald in 1534 and was the scene of skirmishes in rebellions in 1803 and 1916. Red Hugh O'Donnell, Ulster chieftain, made celebrated escapes from its prison in 1591 and 1592. Now much rebuilt, it is a castle only in name.

In the upper yard, under the Bedford clocktower, was the 1552 genealogical office (see page 68) with a Heraldic Museum from which the regalia called the Irish crown jewels were stolen in 1907.

### State Apartments

These splendid apartments provided living quarters for the English Viceroys before the establishment of the Viceregal Lodge in the Phoenix Park. The grand staircase leads to the Battleaxe Landing, named after ceremonial bodyguards' weapons. The Robert Adam-style carpets incorporate the arms of the four Irish provinces. To the left is St Patrick's Hall, with ceiling paintings by Vincenzo Valdre, galleries and gilt pillars. Its name derives from the Order of St Patrick, created in 1783, and the royal standard and colourful ones of 21 of the knights are displayed. The central painting is of George III, Britannia and Hibernia.

Next comes the Bermingham Tower, rebuilt in the 18th century, and the circular supper room with a 19th-century brass chandelier. The shamrock, rose and thistle in its garland can be seen in the ceiling and carpet patterns, which are identical, representing the union of Ireland with England and Scotland. The beautiful, blue, oval Wedgwood room contains a Waterford glass chandelier, an Adam marble fireplace and Chinese-style Chippendale chairs. Also here are three paintings by Angelica Kaufmann, circular reproductions of 'Night' and 'Day' by Danish sculptor Berthel Thorwaldsen, a bust of Voltaire and four black Wedgwood panels by John Flaxman, who worked for the Wedgwood family. This room leads to George's Hall, in the castle's western extremity, which was built as a supper room for the visit of George V and Queen Mary in 1911. It has monochrome chiaroscuro paintings with a three-dimensional effect, by 18th-century Flemish artist Peter de Gree.

The picture gallery is east of here, and its Ionic columns show where it was originally divided into large and small dining rooms and a drawing room. It has portraits of Viceroys and chandeliers of Venetian glass.

### Throne Room

Eastward again is the Throne Room with its heavy throne believed to have been presented by William of Orange, and a huge brass chandelier weighing more than a ton. The ovals and roundels on the walls are by the 18th-century Venetian Giambattista Bellucci.

Next is the State drawing room, which was badly damaged by fire in 1941, and restored in 1968 in the style of the 18th century. It has French silk upholstery, Waterford glass, and a 13th-century Chinese punchbowl adorned with wedding

*DUBLIN CASTLE · RECORD TOWER.*

scenes. Next door, the square Apollo room has a 1746 plaster ceiling depicting the sun god. The room is a reproduction of the back drawing room (first floor) of Tracton House, and the ceiling and mantelpiece are the originals. Behind the drawing room and Apollo room is the State corridor designed by Edward Lovett Pearce, and across it are five bedrooms, two of them designated as 'king's' and 'queen's' and two of them with ceilings from the demolished Mespil House. The one called the Granard Room has a Van Dyck painting of Elizabeth, Countess of Southampton, Louis XV furniture and two solid marble Italian vases.

The castellated stone wall which is visible across the castle garden from these rooms is said to have been built on Queen Victoria's orders to hide the backs of the Stephen Street houses.

The State Apartments were used as a Red Cross hospital during World War I, and can be visited.

East of the bedrooms is the reconstructed Record Tower, one of the castle's original 13th-century corner towers and now one of its few fortress-like features. It houses historical documents and was a prison.

### Chapel Royal

Below the Record Tower is Francis Johnston's Chapel Royal, recently restored. It opened on Christmas Day 1814. On its exterior are over 90 heads carved in

Tullamore limestone by Edward Smyth and his son John. The church's plasterwork, with panels swept down to central clusters of cherubic heads, is by George Stapleton, and the carved oak panels by Richard Stewart, those in the gallery sides carrying the coats of arms of early Viceroys. Arms of later Viceroys are on stained glass in the gallery and on carved panels on the chancel walls. The stained glass in the four centre panels of the east window shows scenes from Christ's Passion.

Excavations in the moat area have revealed an area known as the Undercroft, which is on view to visitors. It contains remnants of a Viking fort, 13th-century tower and city wall.

The castle was handed over to the provisional Irish Government on 16 January 1922 by the last Viceroy, Lord Fitzalan.

### Dublin Civic Museum

*South William Street*

The exhibits here relate to the social history of the city, of which they give a compact overview. There are flint axes, coins from the Dublin Vikings' mint, prints, maps and regular thematic exhibitions. The large stone head labelled 'Nelson' is a remnant of the Nelson Pillar which stood in O'Connell Street until 1966, when it was blown up by extremists. It was a graceful Doric column by William Wilkins, with an internal 134-step spiral staircase, and had stood between Henry Street and North Earl Street since 1808.

### Dublin Writers Museum

*Parnell Square*

Dublin's disproportionately generous claim to some of literature's most significant figures is celebrated at the Dublin Writers Museum, in two restored Georgian houses in Parnell Square. Through exhibitions, paintings, letters, photographs and artefacts, the Museum places writers like Swift, Wilde, Yeats, Shaw, O'Casey and Joyce in their geographical, social and intellectual context.

The Museum also accommodates a special children's section, the Living Writers Centre, as well as offering a comprehensive Irish interest Book Shop, and an antiquarian book search service, lectures and readings.

### Eccles Street

No 7 Eccles Street, home of Molly and Leopold Bloom in *Ulysses* was near Dorset Street where the newer part of the Mater Misericordiae hospital now stands. It was really the home of J F Byrne, friend of James Joyce and prototype of Cranly in *A Portrait of the Artist as a Young Man*. Its hall door was taken to the Bailey pub in Duke Street, and can still be seen there. No 63 was the 18th-century home of Sir Boyle Roche, celebrated clown of the Irish Parliament. No 64, with its medallion copy of Michelangelo's *Moses*, was the home of architect Francis Johnston and later of Isaac Butt, founder of the Home Rule movement in 1870.

Eccles Street was planned as a radial arm of a huge circle of detached mansions called Royal Circus. No new sponsor was found after Lord Mountjoy was killed in the 1798 Battle of New Ross, and the circus was never built. The older part of the Mater Misericordiae hospital (1852–61) is on part of its site.

Playwright Sean O'Casey was born in No 85 Upper Dorset Street (demolished), around the corner from Eccles Street.

### Findlater's Church

See *Abbey Presbyterian Church* (page 34).

### Fitzwilliam Square

This quiet haven was the last of Dublin's Georgian squares to be completed, and is the only one whose central park is still reserved for residents. Its north side was begun in 1791, the west and east sides in 1798. Building was spasmodic, especially during the social decline which followed the 1800 Act of Union, and the square's last houses, on its south side, were not finished until 1825.

This square's houses are smaller and less ornate than those of the nearby Merrion Square, but the standard of finish is remarkably high. They first found favour with lawyers, but for many years now the square has been associated with the medical profession.

Fitzwilliam Square's construction was the final phase of a spate of Georgian building begun in 1762 by Viscount Fitzwilliam of Merrion, on the city end of his sprawling estates.

FOUR COURTS

### Four Courts

*Inns Quay*

Dominating the upper quays as the Custom House does the lower, this great classical edifice is also the work of James Gandon. It took until 1802 to complete, partly because Gandon, fearing a revolution, went back to England for some time during the building. It has a 440ft river frontage and the central pile, 140ft square, is flanked by a pair of courtyards with screen walls punctuated by triumphal arches.

The Four Courts were badly damaged by a bombardment in 1922 during the Civil War; restoration took nine years. The 64ft central dome is not a replica of the original, and purists complain that it rises too high.

The edifice was built to contain the Courts of Judicature, Chancery King's Bench, Exchequer and Common Pleas. It is once again the home of the Irish Law Courts.

The Four Courts site was earlier occupied by the Abbey of St Saviour, a 1224 Dominican foundation, stones from which still exist in the surviving length of city walls at Cook Street. A tunnel ran under the Liffey from the Abbey to Christ Church and most of it still exists, though its ends have been long sealed up.

Father Mathew Bridge, just above the Four Courts, is on the site of the ford of hurdles which gave the city its Irish name of Baile Atha Cliath, and which was the crossing point of Sligh Cualann, the great road from Tara to Glendalough.

### Gaiety Theatre

*South King Street*

The yellow brick façade and ornate 'theatre baroque' interior have a special place in Dubliners' affections. The Gaiety, designed by C J Phipps for entrepreneur M Gunn and opened in 1871, was closely associated for many years with Jimmy O'Dea, most celebrated of all Dublin comics, who drew his audiences from all walks of life. Earlier Henry Irving, Beerbohm Tree, Ellen Terry and Martin Harvey all appeared here. It is noted for Christmas pantomimes, summer variety, seasonal appearances of the Dublin Grand Opera Society and the prestigious Rathmines and Rathgar Musical Society, as well as for other drama.

The Gaiety has survived more than one attempt to close it down and demolish it. Latterly it has been much used for televised shows and its suitability for this will probably ensure its survival.

### Gate Theatre

*Cavendish Row*

This building was designed as the New Assembly Rooms by Richard Johnston, elder brother of the more famous Francis, with advice from James Gandon, and built between 1784 and 1786 as part of the Rotunda complex to provide additional financial support for the hospital. It became the Gate Theatre in 1929. The company had begun in 1928 as the Dublin Gate Theatre Studio in the Peacock, adjoining the Abbey Theatre, with four directors, Micheal MacLiammoir, Hilton Edwards, Madame Bannard Cogley and Gearoid O Lochlainn. The first public performance in the British Isles of Oscar Wilde's *Salome* was among its early productions.

The first production in Cavendish Row was *Faust*, opening on 17 February 1930. The Gate's early years were a financial struggle, with help coming from Lord Longford, who later became a director. As late as the 1950s he was to be seen outside the theatre with a collection box. The theatre now has financial help with an Arts Council grant.

Orson Welles and James Mason were among the actors who gained early experience at the Gate, which continues to stage avant garde productions, Irish and international.

### General Post Office

*O'Connell Street*

This massive building by Francis Johnston, completed in 1818, dominates Lower O'Connell Street and is always known by its initials. It was the headquarters of the 1916 insurgents and the Easter Rising began here with the reading of the Proclamation of the Irish Republic.

The stonework of the building is undergoing an elaborate restoration programme. John Smyth's figures of Hibernia, Mercury and Fidelity have been removed from the pediment on the Ionic portico, and when restored will be used for casting replicas for replacement statues. The originals will be put on display elsewhere in the city. Mortar marks still show where the royal arms formerly adorned the tympanum. On the façade, below a clock surmounted by a harp, the 1916 Rising is recalled. Inside, the main office's centrepiece is a bronze statue by Oliver Sheppard of the dying Cuchulainn, leader of the Red Branch Knights in Irish mythology, with a raven on his shoulder. Its green marble plinth carries the 1916 Proclamation and the names of its signatories.

The front of the GPO has for many years been the recognised site of reviewing stands for parades and of political and other rallies. In an arcade behind it is an official philatelic shop.

### Government Buildings

*Upper Merrion Street*

Not to be confused with Leinster House, the main building here was designed by Sir Aston Webb as the Royal College of Science and opened by George V on his 1911 visit. Parts of it became offices of the Ministries of Agriculture and Local Government under the British administration, and the names of ministries can still be seen on scrolls held by carved cherubs with outsize crowns. The domed building has a rather gloomy ornate appearance, an Edwardian interpretation of the grand Georgian style. Notice that the heavy gate is dated 1922, marking the foundation of the new State.

Across the street the Department of Agriculture's Land Commission occupies Mornington House at No 24. This was purchased in 1765 by Lord Mornington, and is generally recognised as the birthplace of his son, the Duke of Wellington. (He is sometimes said to have been born in Trim, Co Meath.) Another of the occupants of this huge Georgian mansion was Lord Castlereagh.

### Grafton Street

Grafton Street, once an 18th-century residential area, links St Stephen's Green and College Green and is still Dublin's most fashionable shopping street, despite some garishness in recent times. It is an exciting mixture of architectural styles, the shopfronts of Brown Thomas and Weir's being the most distinguished. Bewley's Café (see page 35) is a traditional meeting-place.

Reserved for pedestrains by day, after dark Grafton Street continues to be the centre of a fashionable area, due mainly to the pubs in the streets surrounding it, with their literary and other traditions. In Duke Street are The Bailey, and Davy Byrne's 'moral pub' visited by Leopold Bloom in *Ulysses*. Harry Street has McDaid's, noted for its connections with author Brendan Behan and poet Patrick Kavanagh, and is still something of a Bohemian haunt. In short Balfe Street running from here to Chatham Street, Michael Balfe, composer of 'The Bohemian Girl', was born in 1808. In Chatham Street is Neary's, traditionally a theatrical gathering spot, with one of the finest pub fronts in the city.

### Grand Canal

This 18th-century waterway, which connects Dublin Bay with the Shannon, curves through the city's inner southern suburbs to a harbour near the Liffey's mouth at Ringsend. Since its closure to commercial traffic in 1960 there have been regular proposals for filling it in, but it is a popular and a pleasant amenity, providing almost rural walks on its open banks. A particularly attractive part is the stretch from Leeson Street to Lower Mount Street, part of whose towpath is really rustic, as is the hump-backed Huband Bridge of 1791. Poet Patrick Kavanagh is recalled in a plaque here: he wrote about these 'leafy-with-love banks'.

The nine-bay Portobello House beside Portobello Bridge is a former canal hotel. It was designed in 1805 by Thomas Colbourne for those awaiting the early morning passenger barges which started

from an adjacent harbour (now filled in). The canal benefited from the 18th-century building boom in Dublin, carrying thousands of tons of bricks from Tullamore and Pollagh in the midlands but its passengers were never so lucrative.

### Guinness Brewery

*James's Street*

Home of Dublin's best-known industry, at 60 acres this was until 1935 the world's largest brewery, and is still the largest stout-producing brewery.

Arthur Guinness founded his now world-famous business at St James's Gagte on the south bank of the Liffey in 1759. He began brewing his own porter — nowadays known universally as stout — and campaigned successfully against a discrepancy in revenue rates which favoured imported brews. The oldest part of the brewery lies south of James's Street, behind a 200yd line of brick offices. The original St James's Gate spanned the street and was a gate into the outer city.

A branch of the Grand Canal was run specially into the brewery to enable the stout to be conveyed by barge to Limerick and Ballinasloe, and export consignments to the docks at Ringsend. In 1872 the brewery extended to the Liffey and acquired a fleet of ten colourful and much-loved river barges. The brewery still has a fleet of cross-channel ships, but its internal railway has gone. This had a corkscrew tunnel modelled on the Swiss St Gothard line, and some of its tracks are still to be seen outside the brewery. Guinness's is built on three levels, its biggest single buildings being the giant malt store and the fermentation building on either side of Market Street. The Guinness powerhouse is on the site of the absorbed Phoenix Brewery, once owned by Daniel O'Connell Jnr, son of the Irish patriot.

In 1800 Guinness was just one of 55 Dublin breweries. In this century its biggest

Dublin rivals were D'Arcy's, downriver from it, and Watkins's, both now gone. The Watkins name lives on in Watkins's Buildings, constructed for its workers, a practice Guinness also followed.

Arthur Guinness's grandson, Sir Benjamin Lee Guinness, is remembered as the restorer of St Patrick's Cathedral. Sir Benjamin's son, Lord Ardilaun, opened St Stephen's Green to the public and laid it out as a park in 1880. He also rebuilt the Coombe maternity hospital in 1877; his brother, Lord Iveagh, helped to finance a new wing of the Rotunda Hospital. The Guinness Hop Store in Crane St has been refurbished to house a 'World of Guinness' audio-visual exhibition.

### Heraldic Museum and Genealogical Office

*2, Kildare Street*

The famous home of Dublin conservatism, the Kildare Street Club, once occupied the Venetian-style red brick building at the corner of Kildare Street. Now, the Heraldic Museum and Genealogical Office share the building with the Alliance Française. The Genealogical Office can assist with ancestor searches and with information on family history.

### Hugh Lane Gallery

*See Municipal Gallery of Modern Art (page 46).*

### Iveagh House

*St Stephen's Green*

This noble building forms Nos 80 and 81 on the south side of St Stephen's Green, and is occupied by the Department of Foreign Affairs. It was presented to the State in 1939 by the 2nd Earl of Iveagh, a descendant of Sir Benjamin Lee Guinness, its third owner. Guinness had had the mansion, called Mountcashel House, thoroughly restored.

### Kilmainham Gaol

*Inchicore Road*

Beside a granite courthouse which still carries the royal arms and has a pleasant garden at its side, the gaol has become a shrine of Irish independence. Many political prisoners were detained here between 1796 and 1924, Eamon de Valera — later Taoiseach (prime minister) and then President — being among the last.

Charles Stewart Parnell and Home Rule leader Isaac Butt were among the countless other patriots who spent some time in it. Its major significance, however, is that leaders of the 1916 Rising were executed here and this is what inspired the 1960s conversion of the derelict building into a museum, opened by de Valera in 1966.

Much voluntary labour and funds were expended on its restoration, which included a full replacement of the enormous roof. The gaol, on the side of the small River Cammock, has no aesthetic value. The chapel and cells may be inspected, as may exhibits relating to the prisoners; and the execution yard, which is a thick-walled gravelled quadrangle containing only an Irish flag on a staff and two timber crosses, is also on view. A plaque bears the names of Padraig Pearse, Sean MacDiarmada, James Connolly, Con Colbert and other executed nationalist leaders.

### King's Inns

*Constitution Hill and Henrietta Street*

A glorious classical edifice, built with many delays between 1795 and 1817 to the plans of James Gandon and his pupil Henry Aaron Baker, with some late flourishes by Francis Johnston. Its local nick-name is 'the Temple'. Its fine library, founded in 1787, has over 100,000 volumes including a unique collection of English County histories, but is normally accessible only to members of the Inns. In the park, flanking the doors of the handsome dining hall and prerogative court, are figures of Ceres, goddess of food, a devotee of Bacchus, Law and Security by Edward Smyth.

The central courtyard joins the park and Henrietta Street, first of Dublin's Georgian streets, whose oldest houses date from 1720. It is now much decayed, but there has been some restoration of former tenements. It repays a visit, if only to see how these early Georgian mansions have much more variety in door styles and are also much larger than those that followed. The heavily-decorated doorway and façade of No 9, St Brigid's Hostel, were designed by Edward Lovett Pearce about 1730. Leading architect Richard Cassels designed houses here about the same time. Henrietta Street's popularity with bishops led to the nickname 'Primate's Hill'.

### Leinster House

*Kildare Street*

Now the meeting place of the Dail (lower house) and Seanad (senate) of the Irish Parliament, this mansion (1745–48) was the biggest and most lavish of the great town houses, and its erection greatly boosted development in this part of the city. Its first owner was Lord Kildare, who became Duke of Leinster in 1766. It stands on land formerly owned by the convent of St Mary de Hogge and later by the Molesworth family. The house's similarity to the Rotunda Hospital is no accident, as Richard Cassels used the same basic design for both, to save the hospital's founder unnecessary expense.

Leinster House backs on to Leinster Lawn, which Lord Kildare laid out on land leased from Viscount Fitzwilliam. An obelisk in the lawn's centre commemorates Michael Collins and Arthur Griffith, signatories of the 1921 Anglo-Irish Treaty, and Kevin O'Higgins, Minister for Justice in the first Dail. William Dargan, whose statue is at the lower end of the lawn near near the National Gallery, was a railway builder who organised a great industrial exhibition here in 1853, for which Sir John Benson built a huge glass and steel structure similar to London's Crystal Palace. A statue of Prince Albert survives at the other end of the lawn, though a massive seated Queen Victoria figure of 1908 by John Hughes was removed from the Kildare Street side of Leinster House in 1948, amid amused comments.

Leinster House was sold in 1814 to the Royal Dublin Society, then simply the Dublin Society, by the Duke of Leinster. The society occupied it until the new parliament moved in during 1922, when the RDS moved to Ballsbridge. The public is admitted to the Dail visitors' gallery only with an introduction from a Teachta Dail (MP).

### Liberties

This name applies to about 190 acres in the inner south-west area of the city and stems from a system founded under Magna Carta which gave some areas privileges and immunity from city jurisdiction in civil matters. Each such area had its own manor court. The areas now known as the Liberties are only some of the originals, but are those to which the name has adhered. They also include the districts in which many Huguenots, fleeing from France, settled from 1685 onward and engaged in weaving poplin, originally a fabric of pure silk and pure wool, on such a scale that Dublin became famous for it. A woollen industry followed, set up by manufacturers from England who brought the street names Spitalfields and Pimlico with them. Many Dutch and Flemish weavers moved in and Dutch-style weavers' houses survived in the area until the 1960s.

The Liberties area contains the two cathedrals (pages 36 and 58), Marsh's Library (page 45) and many other places of interest. It also has Dublin's most famous 'flea market', the Iveagh Market in Francis Street, best visited on Saturdays when Thomas Street, Meath Street and Engine Alley come alive with smaller outdoor markets. The Augustinian Church in Thomas Street, with its huge spire, is a neo-Gothic essay by Pugin finished in 1874 and called by John Ruskin a 'poem in stone'. It stands on the site of an 1180 priory. A 150ft windmill tower further west, with a St Patrick weather-vane over its onion dome, is said to be the biggest such ever built in the British Isles. It is a remnant of Roe's distillery, the firm which restored Christ Church. There are two churches of St Nicholas Without (outside the walls) in this area, a classical Roman Catholic one in Francis Street better known as St Nicholas of Myra, and a Protestant one between Newmarket and the Coombe, built by Huguenots in 1707. George Bernard Shaw's birthplace (1856) is at 33 Synge Street.

### Lower Fitzwilliam Street

*'Number 29'*

A picture of middle-class life in the 18th century has been faithfully reconstructed at No 29, Lower Fitzwilliam Street by the Electricity Supply Board (whose reputation for preservation in this area was not untarnished, see page 15) and the National Museum.

The house was first owned by the widow of a wine merchant and paper merchant, Mrs Olivia Beatty, who bought it for £320 in 1794. In a blend of original craftsmanship and authentic reproduction, the atmosphere and furnishings of a typical Dublin home of the time have been recaptured from the basement kitchen and wine cellar through the formal dining and drawing rooms to a children's playroom at the very top of the house.

### Mansion House

*Dawson Street*

The Lord Mayor's official residence is somewhat over-ornate, with balustrade, wrought iron and glass canopy, and a line of eight tall lamps. The exterior paintwork disguises the fact that it is a brick building, built in the Queen Anne style in 1710 by Joshua Dawson, after whom this street is named. In 1715 the Corporation, deciding that the Lord Mayor needed a permanent residence, bought the house and its large surrounding garden from Dawson for £3,500, with no rent payable after that, but 'one loaf of double refined sugar of six pounds weight' to be delivered every Christmas to Dawson's agents if demanded. The first Irish Parliament adopted the Declaration of Independence here in 1919.

The city arms surmount the façade, with the same motif on the side gate leading to the large Round Room behind the house. This room was built in 1821, at Corporation expense, for the reception of George IV. It has a stage and large gallery, and accommodates public meetings, Irish music festivals and exhibitions such as the August antiques fair.

Not all Lord Mayors choose to live in the Mansion House, as latterly a political arrangement has made it almost certain that their terms do not exceed a year.

### Marino

See Casino (page 36).

### Marsh's Library

*St Patrick's Close*

Narcissus Marsh, Archbishop of Dublin, founded and endowed this library in 1701; it was built to the design of Sir William Robinson and opened in 1707. It is the oldest public library in Ireland. The original cages into which readers were locked to prevent stealing still survive.

The collection's 25,000 books include the personal library of Stillingfleet, Bishop of Worcester, who died in 1699, and Dean Swift's annotated copy of Clarendon's *History of the Great Rebellion*, and there are about 200 manuscripts. Marsh, who resigned as provost of Trinity in 1683, died in 1713 and is buried in St Patrick's Cathedral, not far from his enemy Jonathan Swift. Swift blamed Marsh for his lack of promotion in the Church of Ireland, and in 1710 wrote a stinging pamphlet about the archbishop.

The library is open most weekdays.

### Merrion Square

The east side of this, second largest of Dublin's great squares, and its southward continuation comprised Europe's longest unbroken stretch of Georgian houses until a decision by the Electricity Supply Board in 1961 to demolish 26 houses in Lower Fitzwilliam Street and build an office block. The square was originally intended by Viscount Fitzwilliam to run further east and be much bigger than it is. John and George Ensor finished the square's north side in 1764, but its houses have less grandeur than those elsewhere. On the west side the Rutland Fountain of 1791 is by H A Baker, with urns from the Wedgwood works in Staffordshire.

The central park was opened to the public, without too much artificial development, after a plan to build a Roman Catholic cathedral there was abandoned. No 39 on the east side was burned down by extremists in the early 1970s but has been restored. No 73 on the south side is the home of the Irish Architectural Archive, established to gather and make accessible records of Irish architecture from 1560 to the present day. Many of the great names in modern Dublin history are associated with Merrion Square. Sir William and Lady Wilde ('Speranza' of *The Nation*) lived at No 1 with their son, Oscar. On the south side Daniel O'Connell lived at No 56, Nobel prizewinning physicist Erwin Schrodinger at No 65, author Sheridan LeFanu at No 70 and W B Yeats at No 52 and at No 82. George Russell, Yeats's ally in the Irish literary revival, had an office at No 84 where he worked for many years as editor of the *Irish Homestead*. John Bowden's St Stephen's Church (1824) to the east is nicknamed the 'Peppercanister Church'.

### Mountjoy Square

The only Georgian square in the city which is literally a square, this architectural set-piece has suffered most from decay. Its south side was worst hit, and restoration has taken the form of 'façade Georgian' to a large extent, with modern offices behind simulated domestic fronts. Houses on the square's north and east sides have been either better maintained or expensively restored.

The square was built (1792–1818) on a plateau called Mountjoy Fields, and was first called Gardiner's Square. The site was chosen for its height as this was considered healthier. There is a superb view across the city to the mountains from the top back windows of the southern houses. It was intended to build St George's Church (see page 56) in the middle of the square's park, but the plan was abandoned. Tradition says Brian Boru pitched his tent here at the Battle of Clontarf on 23 April 1014; the name Clontarf certainly included this area then.

Playwright Sean O'Casey lived at No 35 and set *The Shadow of a Gunman* here, calling it Hilljoy Square. Timothy Healy, first Governor-General of the Irish Free State, lived in No 1. In Fitzgibbon Street, off the square, James Joyce lived as a boy in No 14.

### Municipal Gallery of Modern Art

*Parnell Square North*

Also known as the Hugh Lane Gallery from the paintings of the Hugh Lane Bequest which it contains, the gallery is housed in Charlemont House, built (1762–65) for the Earl of Charlemont to Sir William Chambers' design. It is a five-bay mansion flanked by curving screen walls with niches and balustrades. Its fine interior is often overlooked, being now a background to works of art. The Earl patronised the arts and founded the Royal Irish Academy in 1785; Samuel Johnson and Joshua Reynolds were visitors to Charlemont House.

As well as displaying art, including modern art exhibitions, the gallery has a regular programme of lectures and classical and modern musical events throughout the year, the details being advertised in the *Irish Times* on Saturdays.

*Hugh Lane Bequest*

Hugh Lane, a nephew of Lady Gregory and a successful art dealer, was dedicated to the idea of having a gallery of Modern Art in Dublin, and donated many fine works as the basis of a collection. When Hugh Lane died tragically in the sinking of the *Lusitania* in 1915, his will was subject to a dispute between the Municipal and Tate Galleries. A long-running legal wrangle ensued, but the present agreement, which runs from 1979–1993 allows 30 of the pictures to remain in Dublin and 8 in London. The 39th, *Les Parapluies* by Renoir, goes to each city on a rota basis.

After the Corporation's acquisition of Charlemont House, a Sculpture Hall and 9 extra galleries were added. When the gallery was opened in 1933 a room was left empty, symbolically awaiting the return of the Lane Bequest pictures.

At the Municipal Gallery, paintings are rehung regularly. The Lane Bequest includes masterpieces such as Manet's *Eva Gonzales*, Courbet's *Snowstorm*, Monet's *Vetheuil: sunshine and snow*, and landscapes by Corot.

Hugh Lane's bequest included important Irish paintings of the period, including works by Nathanial Hone, George Russell, Frank O'Meara, and Walter Osborne, whose *The Fish Market, Patrick Street* captures the essence of old Dublin.

The museum's large collection of works by Irish artists includes Jack B Yeats' *There is no Night*, *A young Breton Girl* by Roderic O'Conor and Louis le Brocquy's *Child in a Yard*, as well as works by Sidney Nolan, Paul Henry, Edward Maguire, Nano Reid, Norah McGuinness and Maurice MacGonigal. The museum has a fine collection of Constables, and a portrait collection which includes works by Lavery, Mancini and Orpen. The Sculpture Hall has works by Rodin, Degas and many Irish sculptors.

### Museum of Childhood

*20 Palmerston Park*

In the pleasant southern suburb of Rathmines, this repository of childhood delights is a charming experience. Its main attraction is a collection of dolls dating from the early 18th century, many of them beautifully dressed, some valued in four figures because of their rarity. There are also toy prams and other playthings, doll's houses and their miniature furniture of varying antiquity, and a selection of rocking horses. The best way to visit it is in the company of at least one small child, and watch his or her reactions.

The museum is open on Sundays and most days in summer.

### National Botanic Gardens

*Botanic Road, Glasnevin*

The Gardens were founded here in 1795 by Professor Walter Wade of the Dublin Society (later RDS). They came under State control in 1878, when they were already quite famous. They now occupy over 50 acres, and while their main purpose remains to promote the study of horticulture and botany they have for many years been a retreat for a public in search of beauty and tranquillity. The Gardens have about 20,000 species and varieties, and are open daily.

Glasnevin's contribution to botanical history includes the first reported attempt to raise orchids from seed (1844), the first successful hybridisation of the insectivorous pitcher-plants (1870) and the introduction to European gardens of pampas grass and giant lilies.

*Main Walk*

Just left of the main entrance, the Thomas Moore Rose is descended from the rose which inspired Moore's 'The Last Rose of Summer'. The superintendent's house, to the right, has one of the few thornless climbing roses in the British Isles. The Main Walk begins at a low greenhouse which contains the cactus and the succulent, aquatic and fern sections. In summer the aquatic section has giant Amazon water-lilies on its pool. *Todea Barbara*, the Gardens' oldest plant, estimated at nearly 400 years old, is in the fern section.

The Curvilinear Range of greenhouses (1843) on the right, among the oldest curved glass conservatories in the world are closed, under restoration 1990–1993. (The oldest, from the same builder, Richard Turner of Ballsbridge, Dublin, is in Belfast's botanic gardens; Turner also built a huge palm house in London's Kew Gardens.) On the far side of the walk is the Palm House of 1884. Next comes a junction, with slow-growing conifers straight ahead and a charming rockery on the right; the Yew Walk or Addison Walk beyond it is sheltered by very old trees, since this, the oldest part, was planted over 50 years before the Gardens opened. It was a haunt of essayist Joseph Addison. Beyond it an area of conifer and beech slopes down to the River Tolka and its mill-race, where are magnolia, cypress and the Chinese Tulip tree. Between the Addison Walk and the mill-race is a splendid tall Sierra redwood. Corsican, Scots and Monterey pine are also here.

Straight ahead are wide areas of ash, lime, maple, yew, larch, elm, holly, hawthorn, beech, hickory, alder, hazel, hornbeam, eucalyptus and other trees.

*Herbaceous Border*

South-east from the junction to the palm house runs the very lovely (in season) Herbaceous Border, with oak and cedar on its right, and beyond that the vegetable garden, herb and lawn gardens, native plants and poisonous plants. The Students' Walk behind the palm house has representatives of the more important plant families. The Chinese shrubbery is near the herb garden.

*Greenhouses*

The Curvilinear Range contains a huge variety of indoor plants and flowers. More exotic is the Palm House with its tall central tropical tree collection and wings for camellias, flowering pot plants and orchids. Small bananas grow in the steamy atmosphere here.

BOTANIC GARDENS

*Roses*

The rose garden with its sundial is in the north-east corner of the Gardens beyond the Tolka. A visit repays the walk.

### National Concert Hall

See *University College Dublin* (page 61).

### National Gallery of Ireland

*Merrion Square West*

The gallery building (1859–64) is by Francis Fowke, architect of London's Victoria and Albert Museum and Edinburgh's Royal Scottish Museum. Some additions, including the rather forbidding porch, are by Thomas N Deane. Paintings assembled for the 1853 Leinster Lawn exhibition formed the nucleus of the gallery's collection. Today the collection contains over 2400 paintings, almost 5200 watercolours and drawings, 300 pieces of sculpture, and the Hunt Bequest of vestments and *objets d'art*.

The Dargan Wing is dedicated to the memory of railway magnate William Dargan, whose promotion of the Exhibition of 1853 led to the establishment of the gallery one year later. George Bernard Shaw felt he owed such a debt to the gallery for the part it played in his education, that he left one third of his estate to it. His munificence is recalled in the 1927 statue by Paul Troubetzkoy at the entrance, and by the Shaw Room, lined with imposing full-length portraits and lit by a magnificent series of specially designed Waterford chandeliers. The original picture galleries upstairs display the paintings of the Italian school from the 14th to 18th centuries.

The contents of Russborough House were presented to the Gallery in 1902 by the Dowager Countess of Milltown. Today the Milltown Rooms display the comprehensive collection of works by Irish artists, including Hugh Douglas Hamilton, James Barry, Maclise, Hone, Lavery, O'Conor, Osborne and Orpen together with a small selection of British art. One room is dedicated to the work of Jack B. Yeats, and another to paintings by Irish artists in France. In the upper galleries paintings from the Dutch, Flemish, Netherlandish, Spanish and German schools are exhibited.

Among the Gallery's notable works are di Paolo's *The Crucifixion* and Fra Angelico's *Martyrdom of Ss Cosmas and Damian*, as well as paintings by Titian, Tintoretto, Veronese, Canaletto, Panini and Batoni. The French School is represented by Monet, Corot, Poussin, Millet, David, Delacroix, Signac and Pissaro and includes Degas's *Dancers in the Dressing Room* (c. 1880). English painters are represented by Reynolds (*The Earl of Bellamont*), Hogarth, Gainsborough, Stubbs, Landseer and Turner. Among Spanish paintings is Murillo's *The Holy Family*, with works by El Greco, Ribera, Goya and Picasso. In the Dutch school there is a fine collection of minor masters plus works by Rembrandt including *Rest on the Flight to Egypt*.

NATIONAL LIBRARY

DARGAN

### National Library

*Kildare Street*

The Library is to the left as one faces Leinster House, and was designed by Sir Thomas Newenham Deane and his son Sir Thomas Manly Deane and built in 1884–1890. Its pavilion and semi-circle of columns are matched in the National Museum facing it, also the work of the Deanes. The Library was the brainchild of the Royal Dublin Society.

It is a treasure-house of information about Ireland, not only in the huge number of books but in magazines and newspapers, many of whose files are complete since publication began. There is also a comprehensive photographic archive. Tickets are needed for reading books, and latterly visitors have been referred for some services to a newer library in the Ilac Centre, Henry Street, so would-be visitors should phone to enquire about access.

### National Museum

*Kildare Street*

The Museum, facing the National Library, was completed in 1890. On the ground floor is a permanent display of Ireland's Gold, which features Bronze Age metalwork, including adornments and fasteners such as gorgets, torques and lunulae from 2000–700BC, together with displays describing the technology employed in extracting and working the gold.

Dublin 1000 is an exhibition which traces the growth of the city in Viking and medieval times, illustrating the houses built, trades practised and the everyday life of the people. It also highlights the influence of Dublin on the Viking world.

The Music Room contains some of the museum's collection of 18th-century pianos, guitars and harpisichords, together with 17th- and 18th-century Irish harps. Decorative arts are displayed in the Ceramics Room, while 18th-century embroidery forms another exhibition.

The Road to Independence deals with Irish history from 1900–1923, and follows events including the 1916 Rising. Here are pistols belonging to Padraig Pearse and Countess Markievicz, James Connolly's blood-stained shirt, the military overcoat worn by Michael Collins at the time of his shooting in 1922, uniforms, flags and banners.

Among prized items in the Museum Treasury are the 8th-century Ardagh silver chalice and 9th-century Derrynaflan chalice, placed in adjacent cases for comparison. The second of these is a 1980 find, and its ownership has already been the subject of a celebrated court case. Here, too, are the 8th-century Tara brooch, 8th-century Derrynaflan paten, 1st-century BC Broighter hoard, 2nd-century AD Petrie crown, 12th-century Cross of Cong, 5th- to 8th-century St Patrick's Bell and 12th-century Clonmacnoise crozier.

### The Natural History Museum

*Merrion Street*

The Natural History Museum is a zoological museum of traditional style which contains a large collection of mounted and preserved animals, birds and fish, both Irish and of general interest. In the Irish Room the display of Irish mammals contains red deer, squirrel, otter and hare. The skeleton of the extinct giant Irish deer is here and skeletons of two whales, stranded on the Irish coast, hang from the roof.

### Newman House

*85–86 St Stephen's Green*

Two elegant 18th-century houses, both owned by University College, Dublin, have been restored and are open to the public. No 85, built in 1739 as Clanwilliam House by Richard Castle has a fine early Georgian entrance hall and one of the most remarkable plasterwork interiors to survive in Northern Europe, executed by the Francini brothers about 1740. No 86 was built in 1765 for Richard Whaley MP and has plasterwork by Robert West. The house passed to Buck Whaley, a celebrated gambler and rake who became an MP at 18 and once walked from Dublin to Jerusalem to win a bet.

In the middle of the 19th century, the houses became the home of the newly established Catholic University of Ireland, with Cardinal John Henry Newman, the great 19th-century writer and theologian as the first rector. Gerard Manley Hopkins, James Joyce and Flann O'Brien worked and studied here.

### O'Connell Street

O'Connell Bridge (1880) replaced James Gandon's narrower Carlisle Bridge of 1794. It is overlooked by John Henry Foley's 1854 bronze figure of Daniel O'Connell in the base of which can be seen the arms of the Irish provinces and 30 figures by Foley, the central one, with harp, representing Hibernia. The four big winged figures, often miscalled angels, are the four Victories, representing Courage, Eloquence, Fidelity and Patriotism as qualities of the Liberator. The bullet hole in the right breast of the Victory facing the Ulster Bank occurred during fighting some time between 1916 and 1922. Above this monument is one to William Smith O'Brien, a nationalist who survived a death sentence imposed for treason in 1848. Following are figures of Sir John Gray, 19th-century civic administrator and newspaper owner, and James Larkin, labour leader famed for organising the general strike of 1913. Half-way up the street is the site of the erstwhile Nelson Pillar (see Dublin Civic Museum, page 39). Above this is a statue of the noted temperance crusader Fr Mathew, erected in 1890 as a centenary memorial. A fountain and sculpture of Anna Livia, the spirit of the River Liffey, is affectionately known by Dubliners as 'the floozie in the jacuzzi'. At the top of the street the Charles Stewart Parnell monument has a symbolic flame atop an obelisk of polished pink granite and a bronze statue (by Dublin-born Augustus Saint-Gaudens) of Parnell, the patriot, whose affair with Kitty O'Shea brought his downfall.

The street is 150ft wide. Its upper part was formerly a Georgian boulevard, Gardiner's Mall, which began the tradition of trees in the street centre. This half of the street lacks public buildings and is dominated by the Gresham Hotel and two large cinema complexes, while the Ambassador cinema facing down it is the rebuilt Round Room of the Rotunda Hospital complex.

Behind the street's upper west side is Moore Street, Dublin's colourful open-air food market, a place of real character.

The lower half of the street is dominated by the GPO (see entry, page 41). The entire street was largely rebuilt after the 'Troubles'. The Ulster Bank, for example, looks Victorian but is dated 1923. Some of the development was regrettable, but it was not until the late 1980s that a special commission was set up to tighten the rules for shopfronts and other displays and restore the street's old glory.

## Olympia Theatre

### Dame Street

The city's second oldest theatre, this became its biggest when the huge Theatre Royal in Hawkins Street, Europe's largest, was demolished in 1962. The Olympia's interior epitomises the old music hall style. It began, indeed, as the Star of Erin music

hall in 1879, but was always popularly known as 'Dan Lowry's', after its owner. In 1897 it became the Empire Palace; a few years later the name changed again. Marie Lloyd, Gertie Gitana, George Formby, John Gielgud, Noël Coward, Alec Guinness, Gladys Cooper, Peggy Ashcroft, Tyrone Power, Margaret Rutherford and Laurel and Hardy have all performed here.

## Phoenix Park

This enclosed space has a circumference of about seven miles and an area of 1,752 acres, bigger than the combined area of London's Hyde Park, Regent's Park, St James's Park, Green Park, Kensington Gardens and Hampstead Heath. It contains gardens, lakes, woods, extensive playing areas for soccer, Gaelic football, hurling and camogie, a polo course, a cricket club, the second zoological gardens to be opened to the public in Europe, as well as the residences of the Irish President and US Ambassador, the headquarters of the Department of Defence, the police force and the Ordnance Survey, and a deer herd.

The park was walled by the Duke of Ormonde in 1671 and opened to the public in 1747 by Lord Chesterfield, the Lord Lieutenant, after whom its main road, running straight for over two miles, was named. The name Phoenix comes from 'fionn uisce', Irish words meaning clear water, inspired by a chalybeate spring which is now inside the zoo. The Phoenix Park racecourse is immediately outside the park.

Inside the Parkgate Street entrance on the right, are the attractive People's Gardens, laid out in 1864. On the right after the Hollow, with its bandstand, is the zoo, with the long building and parade ground of the garda (police) headquarters in the distance.

### Dublin Zoo

The Zoological Gardens opened in 1831 with an enclosure of $5\frac{1}{2}$ acres, little more than a sixth of its present size. It still has an 1833 ticket office. The excellent layout was designed by Decimus Burton, architect to the Zoological Society of London. The society administering it became the Royal Zoological Society of Ireland in 1837 when Queen Victoria became its patron. Today it maintains its large collection of animals through admission charges, subscriptions and commercial sponsorship. It is administered by a council which meets after formal breakfasts, a tradition of which is that porridge is consumed standing up.

Dublin Zoo is one of the few places in the world where lions will breed in captivity, and over 700 of them have been bred here since 1857. One Dublin lioness mothered 75 cubs in 12 years. A lion from here achieved 'stardom' as the MGM film lion. The Zoo includes many birds and a reptile house. Its most celebrated inmate has been a tuatera lizard with a socket under its skin for a third eye. A Haida Indian totem pole, presented to the State by the Canadian Government in 1970, is in the American black bears' enclosure, chosen as a vandal-free site. In a small area of crowned cranes beyond the sealions' pool, a wooden arrow marks the site of the spring which gave the park its 'Phoenix' name.

### Aras an Uachtarain

Aras an Uachtarain is the Presidential residence, built in 1751, enlarged in 1782 and added to again by Francis Johnston in the 1800s. It was then the Viceroy's residence; when the Irish Free State was founded the house was occupied by Governors-General until the office of President was created under the 1937 Constitution.

The most dramatic incident in the park's history took place on the main road opposite this house on 6 May 1882, when Lord Frederick Cavendish, Chief Secretary for Ireland, and his Under-Secretary, T H Burke, were assassinated by a secret society called the National Invincibles; five men were hanged for the crime.

The Phoenix Monument on its elaborate pedestal was erected by Lord Chesterfield in 1747; it is more often called the 'Eagle' monument since the flames which identify the fabled bird are not obvious in the grey stone. Away to the left are the 'Fifteen Acres', an area of football and hurling pitches really about 200 acres. A road skirting them goes to the American Ambassador's residence, formerly that of the murdered Cavendish. Beyond it is Oldtown Wood.

Forking left at the crossroads, a path leads out through White's Gate to the 1835 Castleknock College, in whose grounds is the ruin of Castleknock Castle. Before the college comes Farmleigh, Lord

Iveagh's residence, where EEC Foreign Ministers met in 1975. Past Quarry Lake with its island, a path on the right leads to a house with a private theatre built by Luke Gardiner in 1728. Subsequently a cavalry barracks, since 1825 it has been the Ordnance Survey office. At the next crossroads, the right-hand road goes to the 1864 Mount Sackville convent and school. Straight ahead are the Glen Lake and Furry Glen in one of the park's most attractive parts. St Mary's Hospital, a Cheshire Home, occupies some buildings of the former Royal Hibernian Military School (1766), which was added to by Thomas Cooley and Francis Johnston and had an 18-acre farm where the girls and boys worked.

### Magazine fort

On the right is Chapelizod village where Joseph Sheridan LeFanu lived and set his novel *The House by the Churchyard*. From here a path winds past trees along Corkscrew Hill to St Thomas's Hill and its grim deserted Magazine Fort, which took from 1735 to 1801 to complete. It stands on the site of a house where Oliver Cromwell's son Henry and a Lord Falkland had lived. This fort was raided in 1916 by insurgents and again in 1939 by the IRA.

The road leads between the Wellington Monument to the right and to the left the army athletic grounds, cricket grounds and Citadel Pond, better known as the Dog Pond. The Phoenix Cricket Club of 1830 is the second oldest surviving cricket club in Ireland.

The Wellington Monument, 205ft to the top of its obelisk, stands over 11 sloping steps, the bottom one being 480ft square. Designed by Robert Smirke, it was built between 1817 and 1861, and may be the world's tallest obelisk.

### Powerscourt House

#### South William Street

This stately town house of the Powerscourt family, whose major estate was in Enniskerry, Co Wicklow, was built in 1771 to the design of Robert Mack, who had earlier planned Essex — now Grattan — Bridge, linking Capel Street and Parliament Street. The mansion later became an anachronism, boxed in by commercial streets, but by then it had changed hands, being sold to a wholesale clothing and textile firm as early as 1835 and remaining with them for well over 100 years. Its excellent plasterwork by Michael Stapleton survived this commercial use.

In the 1980s the tall house and its large galleried courtyard running back towards Clarendon Street were converted to the Powerscourt Townhouse Centre, of mainly small, select shops and restaurants, on the lines of a shopping mall but more intimate and sophisticated. The result has been to link the shopping hub of Grafton Street via narrow Johnston's Court with the arcade of the South City Market in South Great George's Street, hitherto somewhat neglected, and create a long, very varied and charming traffic-free precinct. The palatial redbrick building over the market arcade (1892) is a happy coincidence. Henry II once built a palace here.

### Pro-Cathedral

*Marlborough Street*

Designed by amateur architect John Sweetman of Raheny, Dublin, the church's façade with its six-pillared Doric portico is a copy of the Temple of Theseus in Athens; the Renaissance interior is modelled on the Church of St Philip de Reule in Paris.

St Mary's Pro-Cathedral was built between 1815 and 1825 on the site of a mansion of Lord Annesley. It had been decided to build it in O'Connell Street where the GPO now is, but that plan was abandoned for fear of official opposition; yet the design is far more suitable to the original site, as in narrow Marlborough Street one has to go some distance into the grounds of the Department of Education across the road to appreciate the great spread of the façade and see the dome.

In the apse are two altars with mosaics and a memorial window to Sir James Power, a chairman of Power's Distillery. The church is used by Catholics for the religious services which accompany some State occasions, usually with a corresponding service being held in St Patrick's Cathedral.

The street corner above the church on the opposite side of Marlborough Street marked one edge of 'Monto', a red-light district of the early 1900s, written about by Joyce and St John Gogarty and called by *Encyclopaedia Britannica* in those days more blatant 'even than Algiers'.

### Prospect Cemetery

*Glasnevin*

The cemetery wall on the right of Finglas Road coming from the town still has the watchtowers which were once manned by armed guards to deter body-snatchers. The cemetery has spread from its original nine acres to over 100. Burials and cremations are not confined to members of any one religious persuasion, although it was opened in 1832 for the burial of Catholics, as Catholic burial services had run into opposition elsewhere in the city. Below the cemetery the road fork at Hart's Corner is divided by a narrower road leading to an old gate of the graveyard. This gate, long closed, was opened at the suggestion of Daniel O'Connell to avoid a turnpike on Finglas Road at which funerals had to pay tolls.

A replica of a round tower in Dalkey granite, 168½ft tall, stands near the tomb of O'Connell; his crypt and the tower were both completed in 1869, and O'Connell ('the Liberator'), who died in 1847, was re-interred here. The tomb of Charles Stewart Parnell is crowned by an enormous granite rock. This is Ireland's largest cemetery, its oldest and most intriguing part being at the Prospect Square end, inside that disused gate.

### Rathfarnham Castle

*Rathfarnham Road*

The castle, whose grounds border the Castle golf course, has been occupied until recently by a community of Jesuits. A fine entrance gate was the casualty of road widening. The castle was built in the late 16th century by Archbishop Adam Loftus as an outpost to deter mountain men from attacking the city. It had a full garrison in 1641, when part of the city wall collapsed and rumours of a bid to seize Dublin Castle were afoot.

William Conolly, Speaker of the Irish House of Commons, bought the Rathfarnham fortress for £62,000 in 1724 from Philip, Duke of Wharton, who was in financial ruin through cards and drink. It later passed in turn to John Hoadly, Bellingham Boyle, Nicholas Loftus and Lord Chancellor Blackburne. Over the years its Gothic windows were replaced and the Elizabethan battlements disappeared.

ROTUNDA HOSPITAL

### Rotunda Hospital

*Parnell Street and Square*

This was the first maternity hospital in the British Isles to be built as such. It has had worldwide importance as a teaching centre since its inception. Its founder was Dr Bartholomew Mosse of Portlaoise (then Maryborough), who obtained a midwifery licence in 1742 from the Royal College of Physicians of Ireland, which encouraged medical men to involve themselves in maternity care while other royal colleges forbade their fellows to do so. Mosse opened his first maternity hospital in 1745 in the former Madame Violante's Theatre in George's Lane, Dublin, where Peg Woffington had performed, and engaged Richard Cassels in 1750 to design the new building in Parnell Street.

Its biggest visual difference from Leinster House (see page 44), with which it shares a basic plan, is the three-storey tower with copper cupola. Mosse had intended to raise money by having an observatory in this tower. For the same reason, he turned the gardens into a pleasure 'vauxhall', laid out walks and charged admission. Hospital extensions cover these now.

The hospital opened in 1757 as the Lying-in Hospital. The Rotunda, a lofty 80ft-diameter hall from which the hospital gets its present name, was designed in 1755 by George Ensor. It was fashionable in the 18th century as an Assembly Hall, and now houses a cinema.

The Rotunda chapel, over the main entrance hall, is Dublin's most exquisite, with its high relief and beautifully coloured plasterwork by Bartholomew Cramillion, completed in 1758.

Patrick Conway's old-style pub facing the hospital, well-known to expectant fathers, is older than the Rotunda, having opened in 1745.

### Royal Canal

This waterway curves through the inner northside suburbs of Dublin just as the Grand Canal does on the south side. Its towpath may be walked for most of its urban length, from Newcomen Bridge at North Strand Road to the spreading suburb of Clonsilla, about seven miles and further if one likes. From Binns Bridge, in Drumcondra, with its rustic stile, the walk is very pleasant, becoming quite rural as it passes Cabra. Pleasure craft may be used on the water, and locks which had become ruinous have been repaired, entire new gates being made in some cases.

The Royal Canal Company was founded in 1789. Long John Binns, after whom bridges are named on both waterways, was a Grand Canal director who believed he had been insulted by fellow board members for being a shoemaker. He vowed to damage their business with a rival canal, and interested the Duke of Leinster in becoming a subscriber, on condition that the canal would pass Leinster's mansion, Carton House near Maynooth, which it does. But as the waterway, sometimes still referred to as the Shoemaker's Canal, duplicated the Grand in linking the Liffey and Shannon, it lost money from the start. Even its passenger services from Broadstone to Mullingar did not save it. In the 1840s, a railway company bought it to lay tracks on banks owned by the canal, and a rail line still hugs it from the Liffey to Mullingar. A large square pond with swans and waterfowl in a park at the top of Blessington Street is a converted filterbed from days when an arm of the canal provided drinking water.

### Royal College of Surgeons

*St Stephen's Green*

This handsome building dominates the Green's west — and originally least fashionable — side. It was designed by William Murray and built on the site of an old cemetery in 1825–27. It is decorated with a balustrade and ten engaged Tuscan columns. In the tympanum are figures of Greek deities, including those of Medicine and Health. Murray's son, William G Murray, coincidentally designed the Royal College of Physicians in Kildare Street, which was finished in 1864. The surgeons moved to the Green from a hall in Mercer Street, beside Mercer's Hospital, formerly a leper colony. The area between their old and new homes had been the Raparee Fields, a criminal haunt, and as this tradition was slow to die, they were initially plagued by body-snatchers anxious to sell corpses.

The college, now with a large modern extension in York Street, has a pleasant interior, rooms such as the Colles Room being named after former distinguished surgeons. The boardroom has fine plasterwork in its vaulted ceiling. It also has a dent in the copper finger panel of a door, legacy of a bullet fired through the window when the college was occupied by Constance Countess Markievicz during the 1916 Rising. As a colonel in the volunteers she was forced to withdraw there, and promptly asked where the scalpels were kept, so as to use them in hand-to-hand encounters.

### Royal Dublin Society

*Ballsbridge*

The Society's sprawling showgrounds in Merrion Road, flanked on the city side by the Victorian Gothic Pembroke town hall, later a school, were opened in 1879 on a 15-acre site, but the present area is over 50 acres. The show-ground buildings have included the Society's head offices since 1922. They are by George Wilkinson and later architects, and the muted classical frontage on Merrion Road has festooned urns and the heads of sheep, cattle and horses, surmounted by a figure of Plenty in the tympanum over the main entrance. These heads underline the Society's great agricultural tradition; it was founded on 25 June 1731 in the rooms of the Philosophical Society in Trinity College, to improve the condition of the country and raise the status of the agricultural population. Its first headquarters were in the old parliament house in College Green (see Bank of Ireland, page 34), then in Grafton Street and Hawkins Street in turn before it moved to Leinster House, where it remained until 1922. The Society was involved in the foundations of the National Museum, Library and Art Gallery, and it was Dr Walter Wade, Professor of Botany to the Society, who laid out the present National Botanic Gardens.

The best way to view the large showgrounds in Ballsbridge is to attend one of the Society's most famous shows, the Spring Show in May or Dublin Horse Show in August. The latter includes the international Aga Khan showjumping contest, and is accompanied by hunt balls and other social activities in the city. The May show concentrates on farming, with agricultural machinery and other animals than horses. Many other shows are held in these grounds — coin and philatelic fairs, motor and boat shows, holiday and home equipment exhibitions — as well as many concerts and lectures, and there are smaller agricultural shows, concerned only with bulls, for instance; but the two main annual events, with all their sideshows, bring the entire complex into play.

The RDS also owns an exceptionally fine members' library. Beyond the grounds is Thomas Prior House, built in 1881 in curious Victorian style. It is now an RDS premises but was originally a school for the daughters of deceased Freemasons.

ROYAL DUBLIN SOCIETY

ROYAL HOSPITAL

**Royal Hospital**

*Kilmainham*

Dublin's only monumental 17th-century building, this was built between 1680 and 1685 for about £24,000 to the design of William Robinson, Surveyor-General of Ireland. (Christopher Wren is often wrongly named as its designer.) The Duke of Ormonde had ordered its building, at the behest of Charles II, as a home for army pensioners. These, easily spotted in the neighbourhood by their uniforms, were called locally until this century 'Chelsea pensioners', despite their Dublin address and the fact that the hospital was older than its Chelsea counterpart.

The chapel has a notable stucco ceiling and its excellent wood-carvings (by James Tabary) were once thought to be the work of Grinling Gibbons. The building, with a rather quaint clock-tower and four ranges around a quadrangle, has one of the finest interiors in Dublin. It was a police barrack for some time after its original occupation ended, but was extensively renovated in the 1970s and was re-opened to the public as the National Centre for Culture and the Arts in 1985. The Irish Museum of Modern Art was established in 1991, with a core collection of major donations including the Sidney Nolan collection and the Gordon Lambert collection of Irish contemporary art. These are augmented by semi-permanent collections and visiting exhibitions. The museum aims to represent international and Irish art of the 20th century, with associated educational and community programmes. Performances of theatre and music, with a focus on the overlap between the visual and performing arts, are included in the work of the museum.

The ornate Kilmainham gate has a pretentious side tower. Designed by Francis Johnston in 1812, this gate, then called Richmond Tower, spanned the road at Watling Street bridge, near Guinness's, before being removed in numbered stones and re-erected here. Just inside it are two cemeteries; the larger, Bully's Acre, Dublin's oldest, is said to contain the grave of Murrough, son of Brian Boru, and that of 1803 revolutionary Robert Emmet.

## St Andrew's Church

*St Andrew's Steet*

Not to be confused with the Roman Catholic St Andrew's in Westland Row, this church was built (1860–73) to designs of Charles Lanyon on the site of the ancient nunnery of St Mary de Hogge. Its Gothic style, with dominant spire and exterior arcade, is somewhat cumbersome. A crowned pillar commemorates members of the Dublin company of Imperial Yeomanry killed in the Boer War. Across the road, behind the angle of the present Church Lane and Suffolk Street, the Viking 'thingmote' (ceremonial mound), 40ft high and 240ft in circumference, survived until 1661, being levelled to fill holes in what is now Nassau Street. Henry II met Irish chiefs here in 1172.

## St Ann's Church

*Dawson Street*

The church's imposing façade has a neo-Romanesque appearance. Built in pale granite, it is interspersed with single redbrick courses, a style typical of the work of Sir Thomas Deane and Benjamin Woodward, but far more strikingly exemplified in the church's parochial school and hall (1857–58) which stood around the corner in Molesworth Street until 1978. These were the subject of one of the most bitter clashes between preservationists and demolishers, the dispute lasting four years.

St Ann's, now noted for lunch-time recitals, is much older than its façade, and an unusual shelf to the left of the altar in its galleried interior fulfils the terms of a 1723 bequest. Lord Theophilus Newtown of Newtown Butler left £13 a year to the poor of St Ann's parish, to be distributed in the form of five shillings' worth of bread per week. The shelf was erected to hold the bread.

Beside the church is the Royal Irish Academy (No 19), with one of Ireland's finest libraries.

### St Audoen's Churches

*High Street*

Going up Bridge Street from the Liffey and turning left into Cook Street, a preserved stretch of city wall is reached, containing St Audoen's Arch, the last remaining city gate. Steps lead to the Norman west tower of the Protestant or 'old' St Audoen's. Only about a quarter of its area is now roofed. Some historians claim that the roofed part dates from about AD650, others say that the west doorway of 1169 is the church's oldest part. A pre-Norse church of St Columcille was on this site, and some of its structure may be incorporated in St Audoen's. The tower contains Ireland's three oldest bells, dating from 1423, and others from 1658 and 1694. Butchers, bakers, smiths and bricklayers once had guild chapels in the church.

The Roman Catholic St Audoen's abuts the other church and is reached from High Street, which was the main street of the walled city. It was designed by Patrick Byrne and opened in 1846, but the fine Corinthian portico dates from 1899. The church has traditional links with Dublin's Italian community and was sometimes visited by Giovanni Montini before he became Pope Paul VI. Its organ, an early Walker (London), is now a rarity.

### St Catherine's Church

*Thomas Street*

Used in recent times for exhibitions and concerts, St Catherine's was designed by John Smyth and built between 1760 and 1769. It has a broad Tuscan façade and a square tower, and is a handsome but scarcely memorable building. It was completely restored by Dublin Corporation at the end of the 1970s and is an officially preserved building, given a new role as a museum. This church replaces one of the same name built in the 1180s by the monks of the abbey of St Thomas Becket.

On 20 September 1803 Robert Emmet was executed in the roadway opposite St Catherine's, after his insurrection, which included a plan to capture Dublin Castle, went disastrously wrong. A sign on the western part of the church railings indicates the exact spot.

Broad Bridgefoot Street faces the church; to the street's left was the

Marshalsea of 1740, a debtors' prison which later became a notorious slum.

### St Francis Xavier Church

*Upper Gardiner Street*

The church's most striking feature is the Italian high altarpiece, which is Dublin's finest. Its four 25ft Corinthian pillars look like green marble, but are built around timber cores by the Italians scagliola process, using powdered marble and paint. The altar is richly decorated with lapis lazuli. The church has a splendid coffered ceiling with high-relief rosettes, and the side chapels also repay attention. Designed by Joseph B Keane, this Jesuit church (1829–32) was originally intended for Great Charles Street, beyond Mountjoy Square. Its classical façade now stands at the very edge of the Gardiner family's great Georgian development. The church is featured in James Joyce's short story *Grace*.

### St George's Church

*Hardwicke Place, off Temple Street*

St George's, completed in 1814, is possibly Francis Johnston's finest work. It has often been likened to London's St Martin-in-the-Fields, but this is only a general impression, and the differences are distinct. Standing on a street island, St George's is a Greek Ionic gem, with four fluted columns in the portico and a five-storey clocktower terminating in a slender spire, bringing the height to almost 200ft. Inside is Evie Hone stained glass. One is struck on entering the building by its great breadth; the roof span is 65ft.

The church's celebrated chime of bells was presented by the architect. Johnston was a keen campanologist and had built a four-storey belltower in his back garden at No 64 Eccles Street, but complaints from neighbours forced him to part with the bells. St George's received them with a stipulation that they be rung in his honour at certain times in perpetuity. Their sound is still a feature of the neighbourhood on Sunday and Wednesday nights, except at times of repair. In 1836, after their installation, engineers John and Robert Mallet inserted necessary iron arches in the roof to take the extra weight.

The municipal flats now facing the church follow the crescent line of the old

Georgian layout, of which the church was the centrepiece, but 'George's Pocket', the cul-de-sac behind the apse, has not been preserved. Sir John Eccles's St George's (1714) is now only a castellated tower in a civic playground.

### St Mary's Church

*Mary Street*

The unobtrusive church is on a corner beyond Marks & Spencer as one approaches from O'Connell Street. It lies across the top of Wolfe Tone Park, its former burial ground. It became a parish church n 1697 and was soon Dublin's most fashionable. In it were baptised the Earl of Charlemont in 1728, Richard Brinsley Sheridan in 1751, Theobald Wolfe Tone in 1763, Sir William Rowan Hamilton, the renowned mathematician, in 1805 and playwright Sean O'Casey in 1880. Arthur Guinness and Ann Lee were married here in 1793. Dean Swift was a visitor to the church, and John Wesley preached here in 1747.

The church has a fine galleried interior and box pews, with carvings of early 18th-century figures on the organ case. The large ornate window in the east end has Baroque scroll adornments. The big Georgian doorway in the west front is a later addition.

### St Mary's Abbey

*Meetinghouse Lane*

Behind Capel Street and off a street named Mary's Abbey, the lane's warehouses hide the preserved 1180 chapter house of this 1156 abbey. The six-foot drop to its floor shows how levels have risen over the centuries. It is 45ft long and 24ft wide, and has a vaulted roof with groin and crossribs. The mouldings of the ribs, very similar to those in the chapter house of Buildwas Abbey in Shropshire, establish the date of the building.

The abbey was the largest pre-Reformation building on the north side of the Liffey. A cistercian foundation, it had land stretching as far east as what is now Ballybough. Its cemetery now lies under parts of Green Street and North King Street. In this chapter house Lord 'Silken' Thomas Fitzgerald, acting as Lord Deputy and chairing a meeting of the Supreme Council in 1534, heard a false rumour that his father had been executed by Henry VIII. He flung his sword on the council table and renounced his allegiance, starting a revolution which ended with his execution at Tyburn. An historical exhibition is on show in the Chapter House, the only remaining part of the abbey.

### St Mary's Pro-Cathedral

*See Pro-Cathedral (page 52).*

### St Michan's Church

*Lower Church Street*

A Danish church of 1095, almost totally rebuilt in 1686, this has a battlemented west tower and beautiful wood carving. Handel is believed to have played its organ (still in regular use) in 1742, the year of the first public performance of his *Messiah*, which took place across the Liffey in Fishamble Street.

Corpses lie in the church vaults in a state akin to natural mummification; this is due possibly to the very dry atmosphere caused by the magnesium lime from which the vaults are cut, and possibly to the presence of tannic acid, found in oak bark. The church stands on what was the edge of the great Oxmantown oak forest, which is said to have supplied William II with roof timbers for Westminster Hall in 1098.

ST MICHAN'S CHURCH

### St Patrick's Cathedral

*Patrick Street*

The Cathedral occupies the site of a Celtic Church of St Patrick, probably founded by that saint. The sacred associations of the place may explain the presence of such a large building on a marshy site. The River Poddle flows under the Cathedral, making a crypt impossible as water is less than eight feet below the floor. A holy well associated with the saint is now under the park adjoining the building. The first authentic record of the Cathedral's construction is dated 3 April 1225; the common belief that it was begun in 1191 is from older stones which formed a gate to an earlier timber church.

Henry de Londres, distrusting such monastic establishments as Christ Church, wanted a dean and chapter sympathetic to his views, so he raised St Patrick's (the older edifice) to cathedral status in 1213, as it was outside the city walls and Christ Church jurisdiction. Today it is the National Cathedral of the Church of Ireland. The present lady chapel was completed in 1270. After a serious fire in 1362 Archbishop Thomas Minot built the tower which now supports the spire of 1749, bringing the cathedral's height to 230ft.

*The Interior*

The stone roof and four graceful arches of the crossing have been repaired, but never altered. The original groining can be seen here and over parts of the choir, south transept and nave. Beside a Gothic door leading to the robing rooms is a marble bust of Jonathan Swift, Dean of St Patrick's for over 30 years, and over the door is Swift's epitaph with that of Hester Johnson, Swift's 'Stella', on the door's other side. Swift and Stella are buried nearby in the nave. The spirial staircase (1901) going to the organ chamber is modelled on one in Mainz Cathedral.

There are eight bays on each side of the nave, four in the choir and three in each transept. On the north side the three piers nearest the west end are seen to be higher and wider than the others, causing two arches to rise above the neighbouring string course. They are in Cheshire stone, not the original Somerset limestone; this infelicity dates from the 14th-century repairs.

The Cathedral is seen from within to be a perfectly proportioned Latin cross.

*Restoration*

In 1864 Benjamin Lee Guinness financed a four-year restoration of St Patrick's, which included a new north transept, nave roof, middle storey of the nave, south wall in native granite and the addition of flying buttresses. The Guinness firm later laid out the Cathedral park on the site of former slums. It is said that in the service to mark the restoration the Dean began his sermon: 'Today I take my text from Hebrews [he brews] XX.' (XX is a symbol used in grading stout.)

### St Stephen's Green

St Stephen's Green is one of the biggest city squares in the world, and reputedly Europe's biggest. Its central area has been enclosed since 1663, when the west side was a place of execution. Outside the central area, opposite Dawson Street, is a fountain presented by Lady Laura Grattan in 1880. The entrance arch facing the top of Grafton Street is a memorial to members of the Royal Dublin Fusiliers killed in the Boer War, whose names are engraved in its underside. On the west side, a statue of Robert Emmet faces his birthplace at No 124 (demolished). A seated statue (1891) by Thomas Farrell shows Lord Ardilaun, the brewer who opened the green to the public in 1880 and laid it out as the beautiful park it is today. The statue, head slightly inclined, is looking precisely in the direction of St James's Gate brewery. Iron capstans on low granite posts at the kerbs of the green are a reminder that chains hung here when the general public was excluded.

On the south side a seat opposite Newman House is dedicated to James Joyce and his father. Joyce was a student in the Catholic University here. Just inside the gate at the south-east corner is a group of three bronze female figures over a fountain, the Three Fates spinning and measuring the thread of humanity's destiny, by Josef Wackerle. A walk along the east side ends at Edward Delaney's bronze statue of Wolfe Tone.

*The Park*

Entering opposite Grafton Street, the visitor sees a large rough stone with a likeness of Fenian leader O'Donovan-Rossa. Much of the northern half of the park is occupied by an artificial lake, with geese and ducks, crossed by a rustic bridge; on the promontory south of the lake is a 1967 W B Yeats memorial by Henry Moore. Near it are three bronze busts, one of the poet James Clarence Mangan with marble medallion of Roison Dubh (Dark Rosaleen, a personification of Ireland); Mangan lived at No 6 York Street, off the green's west side. Another bust is of Constance Countess Markievicz, the first woman to be elected to the British House of Commons. The third is of poet Tom Kettle, killed at the Battle of the Somme. On the west side near University College Dublin are a bronze bust of James Joyce. A stone seat nearby commemorates Anna Maria Haslam (1829–1922) and Thomas Haslam (1825–1917), in recognition of their work for women's enfranchisement.

A little eastward, a memorial to Louie Bennett (1870-1956), a founder of the Irish Women Workers' Union, takes the form of a small garden for the blind. Instead of flowers it has robust plants that can withstand handling, with metal labels in braille. Beyond the children's play area south of this is a memorial to members of Fianna Eireann.

### The Buildings

The green is encircled by magnificent 18th- and 19th-century buildings. The Shelbourne Hotel dates from 1867, replacing premises acquired in 1824. The Constitution of the Irish Free State was drafted in Room 112. Internal doors were deliberately made wide enough to accommodate ladies' bustles and the hotel is traditionally associated with leading social functions. On the way towards Grafton Street, No 22, with a fine roofed balcony, is the Friendly Brothers' House, No 17 is the University Club; and stone-fronted No 9, where Sir Walter Scott stayed, is the Stephen's Green Club.

The green's east side retains more Georgian character than the others. The Office of Public Works (No 51) with granite Egyptian-style pillars, is notable. Loreto Girls' College, Nos 53 and 54, is a celebrated academy. See also Iveagh House, Royal College of Surgeons and University Church.

### St Werburgh's Church

#### Werburgh Street

The lovely classical façade is part of a 1759 rebuilding; the church had been badly damaged by fire in 1754. There was a Church of St Martin of Tours on this spot before the Anglo-Norman invasion, shortly after which the first St Werburgh's was built. There was another rebuilding in 1662. The present fine interior gallery was designed by John Smith and built in 1767. There is a beautifully carved pulpit, possibly by Grinling Gibbons. A 160ft tower and spire were added the following year, giving the church considerable stature. The tower is seen in James Malton's celebrated print of Dublin Castle. It was demolished in 1810 because of official fears in the wake of Robert Emmet's uprising that it could be used for spying on the castle.

The vaults of St Werburgh's contain the remains of 1798 revolutionary Lord Edward Fitzgerald, who died in the now-demolished Newgate Prison in Halston Street.

A short distance above the church on the same side of the street an employment exchange stands on the site of Jonathan Swift's 1667 birthplace, Hoey's Court.

### Tailors' Hall

#### Back Lane

Despite the unpromising sound of the address, which is behind the south side of High Street facing the churches, this was one of the most prestigious guildhalls in the city. It was unusual for such halls to boast a courtyard. Tailors' Hall, built in 1706–7, added its courtyard seven years later. Most of the weavers who supplied the tailors were based a little to the south of the hall at that time.

The hall's restoration is recent and was inspired by fears that this oldest surviving city guildhall would become a dangerous ruin and be arbitrarily demolished. This had happened to the Weavers' Hall in the Coombe. There has also been widespread demolition of Queen Anne buildings, this hall being the last one or any significance in its area. A fund was established to save it, and it was re-opened as a place for functions. It is now the home of An Taisce, the Irish National Trust.

In the room where the guild formerly met are long, beautifully proportioned Queen Anne windows and the dark timber committee rostrum with its serrated pediment, restored after a search for missing pieces. The building retains the original 'sugar barley twist' Jacobean-style banisters.

## Temple Bar

The Temple Bar area is a network of narrow cobbled 18th-century streets between the Liffey and Dame Street, running from the Halfpenny Bridge through Merchant's Arch, Crown Alley, Cope Street and Essex Street. Once a centre for printers and clock-makers, the area has developed with the flavour of the 'left bank', full of galleries, restaurants, bric-à-brac and specialist shops. The Irish Film Centre has chosen to make its home in the area and developments are planned to make the Temple Bar Dublin's cultural quarter.

## Trinity College

### College Green

Trinity College was founded in 1592 under a charter of Elizabeth I 'for the planting of learning, the increasing of civility and the establishing of true religion within the realm'. The religion referred to was Protestantism, and for many years Trinity was seen in the rest of the country as the mainspring of Puritan Dublin thought. It is correctly called Dublin University, Trinity being its sole college. The first students arrived in 1594.

Statues of Edmund Burke and Oliver Goldsmith by John H Foley stand in front of Trinity in College Green. They were 18th-century college contemporaries. The long Palladian west front behind them (1752–60) is attributed to Henry Keane and John Sanderson, but may have been the work of Theodore Jacobsen, amateur architect of the London Foundling Hospital. The vestibule leads to Front Square, with lawns, and cobbled Parliament Square, whose joint area was the site of the 1166 Augustinian Priory of All Hallows, founded by Dermot MacMurrough, King of Leinster. Its steeple was a landmark to navigators, and is symbolically replaced by the TCD campanile (1852) by Charles Lanyon, near the centre of Library Square. A five-storey belltower by Richard Cassels preceded the campanile.

The Corinthian porticoes of the chapel (left) and examination hall face each other across the near side of Parliament Square, and are the limits of the formal classicism in the Trinity layout. Both are by William Chambers and have barrel-vaulted ceilings and plasterwork by Michael Stapleton, but they are not quite identical. The examination hall, originally a public theatre, was completed about 1785, the chapel in 1800.

Beyond the chapel and set back from it is the dining hall, whose façade, with clock, looks like a smaller version of the college's west front. It was designed by Hugh Darley in 1758 to replace a dining hall erected by Richard Cassels, which had been condemned after several masonry falls. A great fireplace surround in black Kilkenny marble, which Cassels had had carved by David Sheehan for the old hall, is in the common room, over the entrance. Facing the hall across Parliament Square is the science and music reading room (1937).

### The Library

Beyond the campanile, Library Square has shaven lawns, antique lamps and old Oregon maples with wired up branches. On its left is the long grey Elizabethan-style Graduates' Memorial Building by Sir Thomas Drew, completed in 1900, behind which is an area called 'Botany Bay', with tennis courts and students' apartments. On the square's right is the huge block of Thomas Burgh's 1712 Library, which was altered considerably in 1860 by Deane and Woodward. The Long Room, which is 210ft long and 41ft broad, was 40ft high even before they raised it significantly and gave it a barrel-vaulted ceiling. What had been already the largest library reading room in Europe thus became immense.

The Library's chief treasure, the *Book of Kells* is normally kept in this room. A Latin text of the four Gospels with magnificent and intricate illuminated pages, it dates from about AD800. Originally a single volume, it was repaired in 1953 and rebound in four volumes, two of which are usually on display, one open at an illuminated page and one showing text. The openings change regularly. Other precious manuscripts include the *Book of Durrow* and *Book of Armagh*, of the 7th and 9th centuries.

### Museum

Behind the Library is Fellows' Square with the modern arts block and Douglas Hyde gallery beyond it. The eastern end of Library Square is closed by the red-brick Queen Anne apartments called the Rubrics (begun in 1700), the oldest existing part of the college and partly financed by

Queen Anne's grant of £3,000, which she raised by increasing tobacco duty. In New Square are the bookshop and Berkeley Library (1967), built to Paul Koralek's prize-winning design. Beyond that is Deane and Woodward's Museum building (1854), a lovely edifice of strong Ruskinian influence, adorned with marble medallions copied from the ducal palace in Venice. Its interior is decidedly Moorish.

East of New Square is the rugby ground, with College Park south of it. A cricket ball struck from here by W G Grace once broke a window in the Kildare Street Club. A suggestion to build the Wellington Monument here was considered in 1814. In 1775 Provost Hely Hutchinson banned public access to the park on the grounds that it had become a 'public walk for company of the lowest and worst kind', obviously unfit for students who were allowed to play cards on Sundays only.

Back on the north side of New Square is a temple-like printing house by Richard Cassels, built 1734–36. Outside the college, the Provost's house at the foot of Grafton Street was built in 1759. Its façade design is Palladian, and was used for a London house of one General Wade and a house in Potsdam for Frederick the Great. The Dublin example is sole survivor of the trio.

A recent addition to the College is the Dublin Experience, a sophisticated multi-media presentation designed as a complete orientation to the city, which also serves as an introduction to the main events of Irish history.

## Tyrone House

*Marlborough Street*

Now part of the Department of Education, the square granite house to the right of the railed open space facing the Pro-Cathedral was designed by Richard Cassels and built mostly in 1740 for Sir Marcus Beresford, Earl of Tyrone. With three storeys over a rough stone basement, its sombre aspect is scarcely relieved by the six square pillars in its portico. It originally had a Venetian window above the portico, and it still boasts Francini plasterwork and a fine rear staircase.

In the grounds is a white marble *pietà* on a lawn. This is a 1930 work by Ermenegildo Luppi of Rome, and was presented to Ireland by the Italian Government in 1948 in gratitude for post-war Irish aid to Italy.

## University Church

*St Stephen's Green*

Beside Newman House, to which it is linked by a 'floating' canopy over a red-brick entrance which gives no hint of the interior, the church was commissioned by Cardinal Newman as part of his Catholic University. He brought John Hungerford Pollen from England to design it as a collegiate church and it was built between 1854 and 1856. A neo-Byzantine style was chosen, and the architect was heavily influenced by Newman himself. The interior is polychromatic; the canopied altar is set in a deeply curved and highly decorated apse, with an arcaded choir on the left.

The design gave rise to controversy, purists asserting that it was comically unsuitable for Dublin and typified Newman's aloof and humourless character. But it has been generally admitted that the church has points of real beauty.

Since the removal of the nucleus of University College Dublin to suburban Belfield, the church has become the most fashionable place for Catholic weddings.

## University College Dublin

*Earlsfort Terrace and Belfield*

A constituent college of the National University, UCD accommodates most of its faculties, including arts, commerce and physics, in a modern campus at Belfield, on Stillorgan Road.

Some departments are still housed in the older buildings at Earlsfort Terrace. The main block (1914–19) with long limestone façade and Ionic pillars, was designed by R M Butler. Its erection followed an Act of 1908 which made the Catholic university in St Stephen's Green and the Queen's colleges in Cork and Galway parts of a new national university. Earlsfort Terrace was chosen partly because of its nearness to the Green (see Newman House, page 49), partly because an older examining body, the Royal University of Ireland, had occupied buildings there. Earlsfort Terrace's main public interest now is in the fact that part of it has been converted into the splendid National Concert Hall, used for televised functions and fashion shows as well as for performances of music.

# South to North

*This walk across the very heart of the city, from St Stephen's Green to Parnell Square, takes in Dublin's main shopping streets: Grafton Street, originally a country lane and now chic and expensive; Westmoreland Street, which was laid out as a shopping street in 1880; and long, spacious O'Connell Street, planned on a grand scale in 1784 and now alive with ice-cream parlours and big stores. The surrounding side streets and arcades abound in antiques, lace and Celtic crafts.*

*Allow: 1½ hours
Start at the Shelbourne Hotel, St Stephen's Green*

**Shelbourne Hotel** ①. The hotel was founded in 1824 but the present Victorian building dates only from 1867. The four bronze female figures represent a pair of Nubian princesses and their slave girls (observe the latters' fettered ankles). Across the road at the corner of the Park is the statue of the Irish Patriot Wolfe Tone.

*Cross the road and enter St Stephen's Green Park at the entrance behind Wolfe Tone's statue and take the path due south along the railings. Leave the park at the Three Fates Fountain, a gift from the German people in recognition of Ireland's help in relieving distress in Germany after the last war. Walk along the pavement beside the railings, stopping opposite* **Iveagh House** ②. Iveagh House is the headquarters of the Department of Foreign Affairs. The building was constructed

STATUE OF JIM LARKIN

JIM LARKIN

SHELBOURNE HOTEL

in 1736 and in 1939 was presented by the Guinness family to the Irish nation. Its interior is one of the richest in Dublin. A little further down the street is Newman House and University Church, the site of Dublin's first Catholic University, founded in 1854.

*Enter the park again and walk in the direction of the bandstand, cross the central intersection between the fountains and stroll over the rustic bridge, turning left along by the duck pond towards Fusiliers' Arch.* **Fusiliers' Arch** ③. Also known as Traitors' Arch, this memorial was built to commemorate the members of the Royal Dublin Fusiliers who lost their lives in the Boer War of 1899–1900. Their names are inscribed in the panels under the arch. The Royal College of Surgeons is around to the left of the arch.

*Head down Grafton Street, a premier pedestrianised shopping street reawakening to an appreciation of its Victorian heritage. Halfway down the left-hand side is Johnston's Court, an attractive narrow passageway leading to a number of interesting shopping complexes. At the bottom of Grafton Street keep going past Trinity College and the Bank of Ireland, and walk down Westmoreland Street to* **O'Connell Bridge** ④. This handsome bridge has the distinction of measuring more in its width than its length. The building of the first bridge here in 1794 changed the whole axis of the city, transforming quiet residential areas into streets throbbing with commercialism. The lamps on the bridge were once lit by gas.

*Ahead is the* **O'Connell Monument** ⑤. Daniel O'Connell, known as the Liberator, won Catholic emancipation in 1829. This group of statuary was executed by the eminent Irish sculptor John Henry Foley and erected in 1854. If you look closely you will see several bullet holes in the winged Victories: they are souvenirs from the Easter Rising of 1916.

*Walk up O'Connell Street along the central pavement. From here you can best observe both sides of Dublin's principal thoroughfare which had to be almost rebuilt after the destruction of 1916 and the Civil War of 1922. The pride of the street is the* **Central Post Office** ⑥. The building, by architect Francis Johnston, was completed in 1818, and is undergoing major restoration. It is revered as the birthplace of the modern Irish state. On Easter Monday 1916 Patrick Pearse read the proclamation of the Irish Republic from the main door and the bloody rising which followed led to Independence six years later.

The pedestrian street which runs down the right side of the GPO is Henry Street, Dublin's busiest — with 145,000 pedestrians daily — and most popular shopping street.

*At the end of O'Connell Street, at the intersection with Parnell Street, is the striking monument to Charles Stewart Parnell, a leading Irish Nationalist in the 1880s. Turn left here, and then right into Parnell Square West, to arrive at* the **Rotunda Hospital** ⑦. Designed by Richard Cassels and opened in 1757, this institution was the first maternity hospital in the British Isles. The hospital gets its name from the round building, formerly the Assembly Rooms. Its chapel, Dublin's best example of baroque decoration, is open.

*Walk up Cavendish Row. The disused drinking fountain is another example of the city's rich collection of street furniture. Next is the Gate Theatre which was founded in 1928 and has since played an important role in establishing Dublin's theatrical reputation. At the top of Parnell Square enter the* **Garden of Remembrance** ⑧. Opened in 1966 to commemorate all those who died for Irish freedom, this small park is a quiet oasis from the busy streets. The large sculpture is by Oisin Kelly and represents the Children of Lir being transformed into swans. Over the railings can be seen the Municipal Gallery of Modern Art.

*The walk ends here.*

*CHILDREN OF LIR· STATUE*

# The River Walk

*A fascinating tour criss-crossing the River Liffey and the warren of narrow side streets, to see the heritage left behind from the arrival of the Vikings in AD841 to the present day.*

> *Allow: 1½ hours*
> *Start the walk from the Stein Stone, at the junction of College Green and D'Olier Street and head up Hawkins Street towards the river.*

**The Stein Stone** ①. The River Liffey once covered this area, and the Vikings marked their landing with a 13ft-high stone slab. The original stone disappeared in the 17th century. Pass 'Mr Screen', outside the cinema on Hawkins Street, one of several amusing street sculptures you will see on this walk.

*Turn right at the Sheahan Memorial (which honours a policeman who gave his life in 1905 trying to save others overcome by sewer gas) and proceed down Burgh Quay and George's Quay.* **Custom House** ②. Across the river is Dublin's finest public building, the recently-restored Custom

House. The neighbouring Custom House Dock is now the scene of the country's biggest ever renewal project, which will see the transformation of warehouses into a quality development featuring a conference centre, hotel, leisure complexes, museums, housing precincts, shops and light industry.

*Cross Talbot Memorial Bridge and walk around the back of the Custom House (through the gardens if open) to view the memorial and fountain representing*

*CUSTOM HOUSE*

*Ireland comforting one of her fallen sons. Continue around the Butt Bridge and turn right up Eden Quay, past O'Connell Bridge and along Batchelors Walk to* **Halfpenny Bridge** ③. This elegant metal bridge, now almost regarded as the symbol of Dublin, was built as Wellington Bridge in 1816 when a toll of a halfpenny was charged to cross it.

*Cross over the bridge — mind your hat if it is a breezy day — and walk under Merchant's Arch into what is developing as Dublin's equivalent of Paris' Left Bank. Proceed along the narrow winding streets of eating places, craft shops, little theatres and pubs, taking the direction of Crown Alley, Cope Street, Cecilia Street, Temple Bar*

SUNLIGHT CHAMBERS

and Essex Street. Turn right when you reach Parliament Street and walk down to Grattan Bridge and the **Sunlight Chambers** ④. A remarkable little turn-of-the-century building built by Lever Bros. The friezes around the exterior illustrate the labours of men, the merchandising of the raw materials for soap and the everyday use of soap. Their purpose, in an age before modern media advertising, was to promote the use of soap.

Continue along Essex Quay and turn up Fishamble Street. **Fishamble Street** ⑤. This curving road was once the fish market ('fish shamble') of medieval Dublin. In 1742 Handel's *Messiah* had its first performance in Neil's Music Hall — now the iron works of Kennan & Sons.

Turn back to the Quays and walk past the new Civic Offices (the site of Europe's largest and most fruitful Viking excavations) noticing Christ Church in the background. Turn up Winetavern Street and take the next right into Cook Street to see a remnant of the medieval city walls at **St Audoen's Arch** ⑥. This was one of the main gates in Dublin's extensive ring of ramparts and this section of wall dates from 1240. It is worth climbing the steps to the top to view and appreciate the restoration carried out by Dublin Corporation to mark 1975 as European Architectural Heritage Year.

Climb down the flight of steps at the far end of the park and head down Bridge Street towards the Lower Liffey again. On the left is Dublin's oldest pub, **The Brazen Head** ⑦. The present building dates from 1666 but the establishment is thought to go back to 1198. Various insurrections (all unsuccessful) were planned here and the interior still reflects a cosy furtiveness. Traditional music is a feature, especially at weekends.

Before crossing the bridge take in the elegance, across the river, of the Four Courts, complementary to the Custom House further down the river. Walk the short distance up Church Street to **St Michan's** ⑧. This is a historic church in its own right, first founded in 1095. But perhaps it is most famous for its crypt, which contains several disintegrated coffins revealing the skeletons of their denizens, whose skin is still preserved by the peculiarly dry quality of the underground atmosphere. Some of the remains are certainly several hundred years old, and the guide may have you believe that one of them was a Crusader.

Return to the Quays and take any bus (or a 15-minute walk) back to the Centre.

THE BRAZEN HEAD

# The Phoenix Park

*Situated only 1½ miles from O'Connell Street, the 1752 acres of the Phoenix Park contain a wealth of rolling grasslands, expansive city panoramas, shaded woods, curious monuments and noteworthy buildings. This itinerary will cover about an eighth of the entire park, so if you like and you feel energetic enough, you can extend the suggested tour with the aid of the map.*

PHOENIX MONUMENT.

*Allow: 1½ hours. Begin at the Parkgate Street entrance (buses 23, 25, 26, 51, 66, 67, 68, 69 or a 30-minute walk which will take you past Collin's Barracks, the oldest continuously occupied barracks in the world). The road stretching straight ahead for over 2¼ miles is named after Lord Chesterfield, the Lord Lieutenant who opened the Park for public use in 1747. Note the old-fashioned street lamps, still lit by gas, and the decorative cast-iron bench seats. Turn left across the field to The Wellington Monument.*

**Wellington Monument** ①. This testimonial to the Duke of Wellington (who was born in Dublin) is 205ft high and was built between 1817 and 1861. Battle scenes depicted around the pedestal were cast from captured cannon.

Walk towards the road which will take you downhill towards the Magazine Fort. Note some interesting panoramas of the city to your left as you go. **Magazine Fort** ②. Built on Thomas' Hill and the former site of Phoenix House after which the park is named, the fort dates from around 1735 and was used as a munitions store until the 1940s.

Circle the perimeter of the fort and come down to the road which leads up through the Khyber Valley. Take this route and from here on you may encounter some of the Park's animal inhabitants. **Flora and Fauna** ③. The calcareous grasslands support a rare native orchid and a violet. The main species of trees include oak, ash, beech, larch, cedar and cypress. Various hawthorn plantations are widespread. A herd of 300 fallow deer roams between Oxmantown Wood and the Fifteen Acres and you might see foxes, badgers, stoats, hares, rabbits and squirrels. Birds are represented by blackbirds, thrushes, wrens, robins, tits, finches, magpies, jackdaws, rooks and jays; larger species include pheasants, wood pigeons, kestrels, sparrowhawks, owls and waterfowl.

*After walking for 10 minutes or so the towering Papal Cross will come into view. Make your way over to it.* **Papal Cross** ④. The Cross was erected near the edge of the Fifteen Acres for the Papal visit to Ireland in 1979, when a staggering 1,200,000 people gathered here for the celebrations. Even now this is one of the most visited areas of the Park. The Residence of the Ambassador of the United States of America is visible through the trees behind the Cross.

*Moving away from the Papal Cross head towards the main road, passing the entrance to the* **American Ambassador's Residence** ⑤. Built in 1776, it became the residence of the British Chief Secretary in 1782. This late-Georgian mansion was taken over as the residence of the US Ambassador in 1927. A quaint natural stone bridge is visible from the gate.

*Cross the main road by the Phoenix Monument and proceed down towards Aras an Uachtarain (House of the President).* **Aras an Uachtarain** ⑥. Through a deliberate gap in the screen of trees you can see the central portion of the building, which was used as the Viceregal Lodge until Independence in 1922. It was then occupied by the Governor General and since 1937 has been the residence of the President of Ireland.

*Continuing along the*

*path or grass take the next left to the Polo Grounds, past part of the Zoo (you can peep through the gaps in the screening) until you reach the back road. Turn right and walk past McKee Barracks and the* **Garda Headquarters** ⑦. Built in 1839–42 for the Royal Irish Constabulary, this building is now the headquarters of the Irish Police Force and contains a Police Museum.

*Turn right at the first junction and enter the 'Hollow' opposite the Zoo.*

GATES OF ARAS AN UACHTARAIN

**Zoological Gardens** ⑧. Opened in 1831, it is one of the oldest zoos in Europe.

The Hollow is a natural amphitheatre and the Victorian bandstand is still used. From the Hollow enter the People's Garden, go down to the lake, up the steps at the end and walk past Army Headquarters which can be seen through the trees. **Army Headquarters** ⑨. Designed by James Gandon, it started life as The Royal Infirmary in 1788 and was British Army Headquarters at the beginning of this century. It now houses the offices of the Department of Defence.

*Now make your way back out of the Park and walk or take any bus back to the City Centre.*

SEA LIONS   ZOOLOGICAL GARDENS

# Georgian Streetscapes

*Although it has to share space with fine Victorian neighbours and some modern developments, the splendour of 18th-century Georgian Dublin remains relatively intact around this section of the city.*

*THE MANSION HOUSE*

*Allow: 1½ hours.*
*The tour begins outside the gates of Trinity College. Pause for a few moments to view College Green.*

**College Green** ①. This was once the Commons of the medieval city where animals were grazed and the population was entertained by pageants. Trinity College arrived in 1592 and the colonnaded House of Parliament (now the Bank of Ireland) was begun in 1729. In the centre of College Green, with outstretched arm, is Henry Grattan, leader of the parliamentary opposition and an opponent of union with England. At the opposite corner is Fox's Tobacconists — reputed to have been the only shop in Northern Europe where you could still buy a Havana cigar during World War II.

*Walk into Nassau Street and turn right into Dawson Street.* **Dawson Street** ②. A street of boutiques, travel agencies, airline offices and insurance companies. Halfway up is St Anne's

Church (religious or cultural events take place daily at lunchtime); next door is the Royal Irish Academy (founded in 1785 to promote the study of Irish history and antiquities) and its neighbour is the 'Victorianised' Georgian house of Dublin's Lord Mayor, the Mansion House. Facing the top of the street from the opposite side of St Stephen's Green is a decorative horse drinking fountain, a reminder of more leisurely days.

*Turn left into St Stephen's Green and before you turn left again into Kildare Street you will notice the majestic Shelbourne Hotel, Dublin's premier hotel since 1824.* **Kildare Street** ③. This street boasts a fine collection of public buildings. Behind its magnificent iron gates lies Leinster House (1745), one time residence of the Earl of Kildare and now the seat of Dail Eireann (the Irish Parliament). On either side are the splendid buildings housing the National Library and the National Museum. Further down the same side is

SIR WILLIAM ROBERT WILLS WILDE, 1815–1876, aural and opthalmic surgeon, archaeologist, ethnologist, antiquarian, biographer, statistician, naturalist, topographer, historian, folklorist, lived in this house from 1855 to 1876

*MERRION SQUARE*

what was once the exclusive Kildare Street Club; the building is now shared by the Genealogical Office (where Irish family histories can be traced for you) and the French Cultural Centre.

*Turn right up South Leinster Street and into Clare Street, past the old open air bookstalls of the venerable Greene's Bookshop, until you arrive at Merrion Square.* **Merrion Square** ④. This is probably the best-preserved of the Georgian squares. Across the road at the corner with Lower Merrion Street is No 1 Merrion Square, home of Oscar Wilde when he was a child. Walking up Merrion Square West you will first see the National Gallery of Ireland and next to it the reverse façade of Leinster House. Flanking the other side of Leinster House is the Natural History Museum and in front of it is a statue of Surgeon Major T H Parke, an Irish explorer and doctor who was associated with many expeditions to Africa including those with H M Stanley, and the belated rescue attempt of Gordon in Khartoum. The impressive block of buildings in Upper Merrion Street is Government Buildings, headquarters of the principal government departments. Directly across the road, No 24 is the birthplace of the 1st Duke of Wellington.

*Proceed up Merrion Square South and appreciate the long unbroken view all the way up to St Stephen's Church, known affectionately to Dubliners as the 'Peppercanister'. Divert for a while into the pleasant park and view the houses from a different perspective. Continue up to and around the back of the church, noting along the way the name plaques on the houses and the Georgian doorways, each one different from its*

BIRTHPLACE OF THE DUKE OF WELLINGTON

neighbour. You now see the Huband Bridge and the Grand Canal. **Grand Canal** ⑤. Dublin has two canals, the Grand (south city) and the Royal (north city). The description 'inner city' is usually taken to mean the area between the canals. The canals were unused for years but a management plan has been prepared to restore them to a water and linear park.

*Walk along the towpath to Herbert Place and at Baggot Street Bridge turn right and head down Baggot Street. The modern headquarters of the Irish Tourist Board (Bord Fáilte), the Peat Board (Bord na Mona) and Ireland's largest bank group, Bank of Ireland, are situated along this street.* **Baggot Street** ⑥. *Notice the later-styled Georgian houses and the converted mews (where laneways intersect).*

*Continue past the pubs of Baggot Street and Merrion Row to return to the Shelbourne Hotel.*

THE FLEA MARKET

Allow: 1½ hours
This tour starts at Cornmarket (buses 21A, 78A, 78B, or less than 15 minutes walk from Trinity College). Proceed up Francis Street to the Iveagh Market.

**The Iveagh Market** ①. This old clothes market was built by the munificent Earl of Iveagh (of the Guinness family) in 1907 to house displaced street vendors. Here real Dublin characters sell their wares from Tuesdays to Saturdays with wit, shrewdness and a charming style peculiar to themselves. On the outside wall around the corner from the entrance is an extraordinary stone winking face — said to be Lord Iveagh himself.

Continue down Francis Street past numerous curio and antique shops until you reach a street simply called The Coombe. Pass a building with the curious title inscribed on the outside 'Widows House of the Parish of St Nicholas Without and St Luke'. A short distance further up is the gateway of the demolished and relocated

## The Liberties

*These were the areas outside the medieval City Walls which were exempt from local jurisdiction and subject directly to the representatives of the King and the Pope. It was a very cosmopolitan part of Dublin when French, Dutch and Flemish Protestants arrived here in the 17th century to escape religious persecution in their homelands. Due to harsh trading restrictions, the industries they established collapsed in the next century, and the area to this day has never fully recovered from the appalling poverty which ensued.*

**Coombe Maternity Hospital** ②. The history of the old hospital can be read from the plaque on the front of the gateway. Around the back the apt and imaginative names of fondly-remembered Dublin street characters are carved into the steps.

*Turn right into Meath Street, a busy thoroughfare of small shops, pubs and markets, past St Catherine's Church (Catholic) until you reach Thomas Street. Keep your ears open for the rich local accents and turn of phrase.* **Thomas Street** ③. Thomas Street was laid down around 1180 and was once the retail heart of the Liberties that could satisfy all the requirements of the locals; but its position is less important today. On the right is the striking spire of St John and St Augustine — colloquially called John's Lane — an Augustinian foundation. The church was designed by Pugin. Nearer to where you are standing is the National College of Art and Design which functions in a converted distillery.

*Now turn left up Thomas Street until you come to St Catherine's Church.* **St Catherine's Church** ④. St Catherine's was originally founded around 1180 by the monks of St Thomas' Abbey and the present building dates from 1769. Robert Emmet was hanged outside the Church after his abortive insurrection in 1803.

*Keep going straight on into James's Street which is dominated on both sides by the Guinness Brewery.* **Guinness Brewery** ⑤. As you pass Crane Street you can turn up to the converted Hop Store, now an exhibition centre and museum, and relax with a glass in the beautifully restored sampling area. Back on James's Street the main entrance to the

GUINNESS HOP STORE

ROYAL HOSPITAL

Brewery is through James's Gate over which the current year and the date of origin, 1759, are both painted. Take a short side trip up Echlin Street behind St James's Church to see the rear elevations of Guinness and discover the magnificence of Victorian industrial architecture.

*After the brewery turn right into Steevens Lane. On the left is St Patrick's Hospital founded 'for the reception of aged lunaticks' from money left in the will of Jonathan Swift. Further* down the road is Dr Steeven's Hospital founded in 1720 in a district remote from the city in order to prevent the spread of fevers, infections and plagues. Opposite the junction with St John's Road stands **Heuston Railway Station** ⑥. Constructed in 1845, Kingsbridge Station (as it was then known) was a monumental showpiece for the Great Southern and Western Railway Company. It is arguably one of the finest stations in these islands. The Victorian aspect of the platforms has also been retained.

*Proceed up St John's Road and turn left for the* **Royal Hospital** ⑦. This masterpiece was built in 1684 and is French in character. It was designed as a Hospital for wounded and retired soldiers and as such preceded Chelsea. It was thoroughly restored in 1984 and is now a multi-purpose building containing exhibition, museum and function space.

*Return to St John's Road and take any bus to the city centre.*

# Commerce, Castle and Cathedrals

*A tour around Viking and medieval Dublin.*

MARSH'S LIBRARY

*Allow: 1½ hours
Start at St Andrew's
Church in St Andrew's
Street.*

**St Andrew's Church** ①.
Built in 1866 to replace an
earlier church, it occupies
the site of the Thingmote.
This was a Viking assembly
point for civic, judicial and
military decision-making.
The column in the
churchyard remembers the
fallen of the Boer War.

Continue up South
William Street passing the
former Powerscourt House,
now an imaginative
shopping and craft centre
complex. Next to it is the
Dublin Civic Museum. This
street is mainly populated
by clothing manufacturers.
Ahead is the old Mercer's
Hospital founded on the
site of the medieval St
Stephen's Leper Hospital.

Turn right into Lower
Stephen Street and cross
the junction with Aungier
Street into Upper Stephen
Street. Note a plaque to
Dunlop's first tyre factory.
On the right, down Great
Ship Street, are the disused
Ship Street Barracks from
which troops once
protected the British
Administration in Dublin
Castle. Proceed past the
new Corporation housing

and turn left into Bride
Street. Pass Peter Street
where every Sunday
morning one of the world's
oldest bird markets takes
place. Cross the road and
turn right into Kevin Street.
**Kevin Street** ②. Kevin
Street Garda Station was
formerly the medieval
Archbishops' Palace of St
Sepulchre. The present
gateposts, a coat-of-arms,
a window, an internal door
and the thick walls remain
from this period. Directly
across the road and up a
short lane is the Cabbage
Garden: now a beautiful
park, this was once a
Huguenot cemetery. Their
historic headstones are still
neatly displayed. The
Deanery, where Jonathan
Swift lived, is divided from
the police station by St
Patrick's Close.

Turn into St Patrick's
Close. Note the old horse
trough against the footpath,
and Marsh's Library and St
Patrick's Cathedral ahead.
**Marsh's Library** ③.
Founded in 1701 by
Archbishop Marsh, it is the
oldest public library in
Ireland, with books dating
back to 1472. The patrons'
reading cages (to prevent
pilferage) are still in place.
**St Patrick's Cathedral** ④.
This ancient and famous
cathedral would have

collapsed from disrepair
but for the generosity of
brewer Sir Benjamin Lee
Guinness who restored it in
the 1860s. His statue is just
inside the railings next to
the entrance. The
atmosphere created by the
bells of St Patrick's and by
nearby Christ Church is
worth savouring any
Sunday.

Turn right into Patrick
Street passing St Patrick's
Park where just inside the
gate is a small plaque
indicating the site of St
Patrick's Well, where the
saint is reputed to have
baptised the locals. Next to
the park is a housing
complex which includes the
ornate, formerly Bull Alley
Play Centre. The Guinness
family built all of this and
laid out the park for the
poor of Dublin. Cross the
road and enter Back Lane
to view **Tailors' Hall** ⑤,
the headquarters of An
Taisce, the National Trust
for Ireland. It is one of
Dublin's few remaining
Queen Anne buildings
(erected in 1706) and is the
city's oldest surviving
guildhall. It retains many of
its original features.

Leave Back Lane and
cross over High Street (the
old Viking main street) to
compare the 12th-century
Protestant church with its

Catholic counterpart (mid-19th century). Both are named after St Audoen. The difference between street levels separated by seven centuries is visible through a window in the Catholic churchyard.

Walk towards Christ Church, first passing the Synod Hall, now a tourist and community centre (its tower dates from an earlier church). Notice the connecting arched walkway with the cathedral itself. **Christ Church** ⑥. The excavated ruins beside the main door are the remains of an Augustinian Priory suppressed after the Reformation. Built in the late 12th century this great

OLYMPIA THEATRE

CHRIST CHURCH

edifice also faced ruin in the last century and was saved by the distiller, Henry Roe. The crypt, perhaps Dublin's oldest existing structure, dates from 1172.

Leave Christ Church and cross the road, with a view of St Werburgh's Church, and enter Castle Street. Ahead is the City Hall and to the right, **Dublin Castle** ⑦. Begun by King John in 1204, it has been much altered. Recent years have seen millions of pounds

spent on restoring Dublin Castle to its earlier elegance, with a view to making it Ireland's centre for EEC Presidency sessions.

After the castle, view in turn the City Hall, the Sick and Indigent Roomkeepers' Society building (Dublin's oldest charity) in Palace Street and the Olympia Theatre across the road. Walk into Dame Street to see some notable financial institutions, including the modern Central Bank which caused a furore when it was built in the 1970s.

The walk ends outside Trinity College.

# DIRECTORY

Transport, accommodation, eating out,
traditional pubs, entertainment,
what to see, where to shop, sports,
useful information

# Using the Directory

The following pages contain practical information including addresses, telephone numbers and opening times. Any prices are approximate and in Irish currency.

**Addresses in Dublin**

The postal district number is given after the street name. Odd postal numbers (1, 3, 5 etc) are north of the city, even numbers are south.

**Telephone Numbers**

Dublin numbers are given in six- or seven-figures, and some are currently being changed to seven figures. If calling Dublin from elsewhere in Ireland, use the prefix 01 before the number. If calling from outside Ireland, use the appropriate international dialling code (e.g. 010 353 1 from the UK).

The information in this directory is liable to change at short notice. While every effort has been made to ensure that it is comprehensive and up to date, the publishers cannot accept responsibility for errors or omissions, or for changes in the details given.

# How to Get There

Dublin Airport is served by major international airlines from the United Kingdom, Europe and North America, and has internal flights. Competition between airlines makes short trips feasible — for golf, fishing or sightseeing — as well as longer holidays. The airport is about seven miles from the city centre and is served by the 41A bus or the Airport Bus Service

from the Central Bus Station (Busaras).

Both the B & I Line and Sealink operate daily cross channel ferry services between Dublin and Britain. Their passenger offices are in Westmoreland Street, Dublin 2. For B & I information, telephone 778271; Sealink 808844.

**Entry Requirements**

Visas are not generally required to get into Ireland except from a small number of countries such as the USSR, Cuba and Libya. Anyone coming from a place outside the State, other than Great Britain or Northern Ireland, must be in possession of a valid passport or other document of equal validity.

# Accommodation

If you come for the Horse Show, then a Dublin 4 address will probably get you closest; for shopping and city centre sights, Dublin 1 and 2 (central addresses north and south of the Liffey) will be convenient. A Room Reservation Service is provided by Dublin & East Tourism.

Hotels listed with stars are AA recommended. Those shown without stars are not AA listed but are established hotels of reputation.

The *Hostels* listed here are not AA recommended, but are approved by the Tourist Board. They are included as accepted basic accommodation.

**AA Classification**

★★    Hotels with a good standard of accommodation. There should be

20% private bathrooms or showers

★★★    Well-appointed hotels. Two thirds of the bedrooms should have private bathrooms or showers

★★★★    Exceptionally well-appointed hotels offering high standards of comfort and service. All bedrooms should have private bathrooms or showers

T & C    Town and Country Homes are regularly inspected and meet minimum criteria

**Restaurants**

| | |
|---|---|
| X | Modest but good |
| XX | Higher standard of comfort than above |
| XXX | Well-appointed |
| XXXX | Exceptionally well-appointed restaurant |

Rosettes indicate that the cuisine is of a higher standard than is expected in an establishment within the classification. Red stars indicate outstanding merit within the classification.

For more details and latest information on hotels, guesthouses and restaurants please see the current edition of the *AA Members' Handbook — Ireland*, and *AA Hotels and Restaurants in Britain & Ireland*.

## HOTELS

**Berkeley Court**
Lansdowne Rd, 4 ☎601711

★★★★**Burlington** Leeson St, 4 ☎605222

★★★★**Conrad** Earlsfort Terrace, 2 ☎765555

★★★★**Jury's** Ballsbridge, 4 ☎605000

★★★★(red stars) **Shelbourne** St Stephen's Green, 2 ☎766471

**Westbury** off Grafton St, 2 ☎6791122

★★★**Ashling** Parkgate St, 8 ☎772324

★★★**Blooms** Anglesea St, 2 ☎715622

★★★**Central** 1–5 Exchequer St, 2 ☎6797302

★★★**Dublin International** (at Dublin Airport) ☎379211

★★★**Green Isle** Clondalkin, 22 ☎593406

**Gresham** O'Connell St, 1 ☎746881

★★**Longfield's** Fitzwilliam St, 2 ☎761367

★★★**Hotel Montrose** Stillorgan Rd, 4 ☎269331

★★★**Marine** (at Sutton 8m N on coast road R106) ☎322613

★★★**Royal Dublin** O'Connell St, 1 ☎733666

★★★**Skylon** Upr Drumcondra Rd, 9 ☎379121

★★★**Stephen's Hall** 14/17 Lower Leeson St, 2 ☎610585

★★★**Tara Tower** Merrion Rd, 4 ☎2694666

### DUN LAOGHAIRE
★★★**Royal Marine** ☎801911

★★★**Hotel Victor** Rochestown Av. ☎853555

### HOWTH
★★**Howth Lodge** ☎321010

### KILLINEY
★★★**Court** ☎2851622

★★★**Fitzpatrick's Castle** ☎2840700

### MALAHIDE
★★★**Grand** ☎450633

## GUESTHOUSES

**Ariel House** 52 Lansdowne Rd, 4 ☎685512

**Beddington** 181 Rathgar Rd, 6 ☎978047

**Egan's** 7 Iona Pk, 9 ☎303611

**Georgian House** 20 Lr Baggot St, 2 ☎618832

**Iona House** 5 Iona Pk, 9 ☎306217

**Mount Herbert** 7 Herbert Rd, 4 ☎684321

**St Aidan's** 32 Brighton Rd, 6 ☎902011/906178

**T & C Bective House** 2 Eglinton Ter, Donnybrook, 4 ☎692983

**T & C Marelle** 92 Rathfarnham Rd ☎904690

### DUN LAOGHAIRE

**T & C Ferry** 15 Clarinda Pk N ☎2808301

**T & C Tara Hall** 24 Sandycove Rd ☎805210

## HOSTELS

**An Óige** The Irish Youth Hotel Association, 39 Mountjoy Sq, 1 ☎363111

**Hostel** at 61, Mountjoy Street ☎301766. Open all year. Self-catering kitchens and restaurant.

## OTHER HOSTELS

Tourist Board approved:

**YWCA Radcliffe Hall** St John's Rd, Sandymount, 4 ☎694521 More a good-value guesthouse; Bus No 3 goes to the door. Open all year except Xmas

**Isaac's** The Dublin Tourist Hostel, 2–5 Frenchman's Lane, 1 ☎749321/787227 Self-catering kitchens and restaurant. Open all year, 24 hours a day

**The Young Traveller** St Mary's Place, 7 ☎305000/305319 4-bedded rooms, each with shower, towels, soap, sheets and duvet supplied; coin-operated launderette, TV lounge. Open all year, 24 hours a day

# Eating and Drinking Out

The most memorable Irish meals are likely to be those which have been cooked with care and respect for their incomparable raw ingredients and will probably have one or other of the following in them somewhere: shellfish, smoked salmon, fresh salmon (January to August), sea trout, roast beef, fresh brown bread, hot scones.

Pubs are as much a part of Irish life as churches and betting shops, and more than anything else in this country attract an astonishing cross-section of people.

The pubs in this list are all traditional in the sense that Dubliners gather in them as a matter of course. But a listing such as this must be subjective.

The *restaurants* listed here are AA recommended. The *pubs* and *coffee shops* which follow are not AA recommended, but are included as traditional and acceptable Dublin venues. Restaurants come first.

⊕ ✕✕✕✕✕**Le Coq Hardi** 35 Pembroke Rd, 4 ☎689070

⊕✕✕✕**Celtic Mews** 109a Lower Baggot St, 2 ☎760796

⊕✕✕✕**Ernie's Mulberry Gdns** Donnybrook, 4 ☎693300

**The Grey Door** 23 Upper Pembroke Rd ☎763286

✕✕✕**Killakee House** Killakee Rd, Rathfarnham ☎932645

✕✕✕**Locks** 1 Windsor Ter, 8 ☎543391

⊕ ✕✕✕**The Lord Edward** 23 Christchurch Pl, 8 ☎542420

**Mitchell's Cellars** 21 Kildare St, 2 ☎680367

⊕ ✕✕✕**Patrick Guilbaud** 46 James's Pl, 2 ☎764192

XXDobbin's Wine Bistro 15 Stephen's Ln, 2 ☎764679

XXEastern Tandoori 34/5 S William St, 2 ☎710428

XXKapriol 45 Lower Camden St, 2 ☎751235

XXLes Frères Jacques 74 Dame St, 2 ☎794555

XXOld Dublin 91 Francis St, 8 ☎542028

⊛XXPigalle 14 Temple Bar, 2 ☎719262

XXRajdoot Tandoori Westbury Centre, Clarendon St, 2 ☎6794274

XCoffers 6 Cope St, 2 ☎715740

DALKEY
XXGuinea Pig ☎859055

DUN LAOGHAIRE
⊛XXXRestaurant Na Mara Crofton Rd ☎806767

XXPier 3 Marine Pde ☎842234

HOWTH
⊛XXXKing Sitric ☎325235

### TRADITIONAL PUBS

An Béal Bocht 58 Charlemont St, 2. Traditional music nights; probably the only cash register in the city that gives receipts in Irish.

The Bailey Duke St, 2

Brazen Head Inn 20 Lr Bridge St, 8. First got its licence in 1666; probably the oldest pub in the city.

Davy Byrne's 21 Duke St, 2. A stopping point in Leopold Bloom's trek on 16 June 1904.

Doheny & Nesbitts 5 Lr Baggot St, 2. Complete with 'snugs'; attracts barristers, journalists, fiercely loyal regulars.

Joxer Daly's 103 Dorset St, 1. Lovely pub noted for its lunches and snacks.

Kitty O'Shea's 23 Upper Grand Canal St, 4. Delightful-looking pub with traditional music nights. Good Sunday breakfasts.

McDaid's Harry St, 1. A famous literary drinking spot for Dublin's bygone literati; now full of types who always have a book in progress but never seem to finish.

Mulligan's 8 Poolbeg St, 2. Looks its 200 years; ambience lends itself to an extraordinary sampling of Irish life.

Neary's 1 Chatham St, 1. Not everyone's idea of a traditional pub but comfortably plush and central, with excellent sandwiches.

O'Donoghue's 15 Merrion Row, 2. The king of all traditional pubs with music of the 'bring your own' variety; one of the most genial hosts in the country.

The Old Stand 37 Exchequer St, 2. Backslapping sporty types; lovely pub.

William Ryans 28 Parkgate St, 8. Beautifully fitted pub off the beaten track.

Scruffy Murphy's 1 Powerscourt, Lr Mount St, 2. Stylish mix of sociable singles and regulars.

Slattery's 129 Capel St, 2. A favourite for music enthusiasts; traditional, folk and blues.

The Stag's Head 1 Dame Court, 2. Difficult to find but worth it — best approached from Exchequer St. A relaxed 200-year-old pub and a large cast of regulars.

Toner's Victorian Bar 139 Lr Baggot St, 2. Highly sociable mix of students and artists.

### COFFEE SHOPS

Bewley's 78/79 Grafton St, 2; 12 Westmoreland St, 2; 13 South Great George's St, 2. Dublin's best-known rendezvous; irresistible aroma of coffee beans.

Club '76 Brown Thomas of Grafton St, 2. Good coffee; excellent gateaux.

The Kilkenny Shop Nassau St, 2. Bright, airy café overlooking Trinity College's cricket ground; notable brown bread and salads.

Municipal Gallery of Modern Art Parnell Sq. Good mix of people, excellent soup; open during gallery hours.

National Gallery Restaurant Merrion Sq, 2. Popular lunch and snack venue; open during gallery hours.

Next Henry St, 1. Coffee counter inside the door; good vantage point from which to watch the motley pass.

The Shelbourne Hotel St Stephen's Green, 2. Elegant stopping-point for morning coffee, afternoon tea; good for celebrity-spotting.

# Places to Visit

Dublin city is a gift for anybody who likes walking and has time to spare. A large part of the city's attraction lies in its people; the warmth of the true 'Dubs', their gregariousness and willingness to help, are just as much a part of Dublin as Christ Church or Trinity College.
A popular way of seeing

Dublin is through guided walks. Contact: Guided Walks into Old Dublin (Liberties), conducted by native Dubliners ☎533423/ 532407. Tour Guides Ireland, 12, Parliament St ☎6794291.
Old City, Georgian and Cultural Trails are self-guided with leaflets and signed routes. The Rock'n Stroll tour appeals to those with an

interest in U2, Bob Geldof and Dublin's 20th-century musical figures.
In the listings which follow, brief descriptions are usually given only for city centre places not elsewhere in the book. Otherwise, see pages 34–61 for more information on places in central Dublin. Admission is free except where stated.

## ARCHAEOLOGY

**Wood Quay,** 8. Cradle of the city of Dublin, key to its Viking past, pulse of Viking city life between the 9th and 11th centuries, Wood Quay is now the site of blocks of civic offices, not erected without a struggle. The excavations revealed a mighty store of Viking artefacts, which may be viewed in the National and Civic Museums. Open any time.

### OUTSIDE DUBLIN

**Newgrange** Co Meath (Boyne Valley). Open Jun–Sep, daily; Nov–Mar, Tue–Sat & Sun pm. Admission charge. Booking advisable.

**Knowth** Co Meath (Boyne Valley). Open Jun–Sep, 9.30am–6.30pm daily. Admission charge.

## ART GALLERIES

**Chester Beatty Library & Gallery of Oriental Art** 20 Shrewsbury Rd, 4 ☎692386. Open Tue–Fri 10am–5pm, Sat 2–5pm. Free guided tours Wed & Sat, 2.30.

**Hugh Lane Municipal Gallery of Modern Art** Charlemont Ho, Parnell Sq, 1 ☎741903. Open Tues–Fri 9.30am–6pm, Sat 9.30–5, Sun 11–5.

**Irish Museum of Modern Art** Royal Hospital, Kilmainham, 8 ☎718666. Open Tue–Sun 10am–5.30pm.

**National Gallery of Ireland** Merrion Sq West, 1 ☎615133. Open weekdays 10am–6pm, Thu til 9pm; Sun 2–5pm (& guided tours). Special bookings through Education Officer 2wks in advance. Bookshop & restaurant. Admission free.

**Royal Hibernian Academy Gallagher Gallery** Ely Place, 2 ☎612558. Open Mon–Sat 11am–5pm, Thurs 11–9, Sun 2–5.

**United Arts Club 3** Upr Fitzwilliam St, 2 ☎762965. Paintings by Irish artists. Open lunchtime and evenings; evenings only at weekends.

### OUTSIDE DUBLIN

**Portrait Gallery** Malahide Castle, Malahide, Co Dublin ☎452337/452655. Open Mon–Fri 10am–12.45, 2–5pm; Apr–Oct, Sat 11am–6pm, Sun & BHs 2–6pm; Nov–Mar, Sat, Sun, BHs 2–5pm. Restaurant. Admission charge.

## COMMERCIAL GALLERIES

Dublin has numerous examples: see Bord Fáilte Information Sheet No 37.

## CATHEDRALS AND CHURCHES

Churches are open for services and at the times given below. They may be open at other times, but these are liable to change.

**Abbey Presbyterian Church** Parnell Square, 1. Open for services (11am Sun).

**Christ Church Cathedral** Lord Edward St, 8. Open 10am–pm except during services; Sun 11am sung Eucharist, 3.30 Choral evensong.

**Pro-Cathedral** Marlborough St, 1. Mass is sung each Sunday at 11am; 5.05 sung vespers by boys of the Palestrina Choir.

**St Andrew's Church** St Andrew's St, 2. Open for services, 12.00 noon.

**St Ann's Church,** Dawson St, 2. Open daily, all year. Admission charge for lunchtime recitals.

**St Audoen's Church,** High St, 8. Visits by arrangement with Rector. Services 10.45am.

**St Catherine's Church** Thomas St, 2. Not open.

**St Francis Xavier Church** Gardiner St, 1. Open for services.

**St George's Church** Hardwick Pl, off Temple St, 1. Not open, but sometimes used as a theatre.

**St Mary's Church** Mary St, 1. Check with Tourist Information Centre.

**St Mary's Pro-Cathedral** (see Pro-Cathedral).

**St Michan's Church** Church St, 8. Tours of church & vaults Mon–Fri 10am–12.45pm, 2–4.45pm; Sat 10am–12.45pm. Vaults closed Sun & Easter. Sunday service 11.45am. Admission charge.

**St Patrick's Cathedral** Patrick St, 2. Open Mon–Fri 9am–6pm, Sat 9am–4pm, Sun at times of Divine Service. 11.45 sung Eucharist, 3.15 sung evensong with choristers from Cathedral Choir School, founded 1432.

**St Werburgh's Church** Werburgh St (off Christ Church Place), 8 ☎720673. Open Mon–Fri 10am–4pm by appointment. Sunday service 10.30am.

**University Church** St Stephen's Green, 2. Open for services daily.

## CEMETERIES

**Arbour Hill Cemetery** Arbour Hill, 7. Scene of many sombre wreath-laying occasions: the executed leaders of the Easter Rising in 1916 are buried here. Open daily 9.30am–5.30pm.

**Prospect Cemetery** Glasnevin, 9. Open daily.

## HISTORIC BUILDINGS

'Not open' means that the building is not generally open to the public, although it is worth seeing from outside and may be open for functions or by invitation.

**Bank of Ireland** College Green, 2 ☎615933. Open banking hours Mon–Fri. Guided tours to the House of Lords.

**Belvedere House** Visits by arrangement with Rector ☎744795.

**Bluecoat School** Not open.

**Casino** Malahide Road, Marino. Open 10am–6.30pm mid Jun–Sep. Admission charge.

**City Hall** Dame St, 2. Open Mon–Fri 9am–1, 2.15–5pm.

**Custom House** Not open.

**Drimnagh Castle** 13th-century moated castle. Open Sun 2–5pm.

**Dublin Castle** Dame St, 2 ☎6793713. Usually open Mon–Fri 10am–12.15pm and 2pm–5pm, Sat and Sun 2pm–5pm. Admission charge.

**Four Courts** Inns Quay, 8 ☎725555. Open Mon–Fri 11am–1pm, 2–4pm.

**General Post Office** (GPO) O'Connell St, 1 ☎726666. Open for business Mon–Sat 8am–8pm, Sun 10am–6.30pm

**Government Buildings** Not open.

**Guinness Hop Store** (see *Museums*)

**Irish Whiskey Corner** Irish Distillers, Bow St, 7 ☎725566. Old warehouse converted into exhibition centre with a relaxing bar for tasting sessions. The selling is indeed persuasive and Scotch-drinkers may be converted in spite of themselves. Party tours. Take buses 21 or 78, or a taxi.

**Iveagh House** Not open.

**Kilmainham Gaol Historical Museum** Kilmainham, 8 ☎535984. Open Jun–Sep 11am–6pm, Oct–May 2–6pm, Sun, Wed, BHs. Admission charge.

**King's Inns** Constitution Hill and Henrietta St, 1. The park is open to the public. The building and library may be visited by arrangement with one of the Benchers of King's Inns.

**Leinster House** Kildare St and Merrion Sq, 2 ☎789911. The public is admitted to the Dail visitors' gallery only with an introduction from a Teachta Dáil (MP) or on production of a passport.

**Mansion House** Not open.

**Newman House** St Stephen's Green, 2 ☎757255. Open May–Oct Tue–Fri 10am–4pm; Sat 2–4.30pm; Sun 11am–2pm. Admission charge.

**Rathfarnham Castle** Not open.

**Rotunda Hospital** Parnell St and Sq, 1 ☎730700. Parties may visit chapel by arrangement.

**Royal College of Surgeons** Not open.

**The Royal Hospital** Kilmainham, 8 ☎718666. Guided tours, concerts, exhibitions, etc. Restaurant. Admission charge.

**Tailors' Hall** Not open.

**Trinity College, 2** ☎772941. Trinity belongs to all the people of Dublin and the grounds are a favourite place for a lunchtime run or just for sunbathing. *The Book of Kells* may be found in the Long Room of the Old Library; queues to see it are often horrendous. *The Book of Kells*: open Mon–Fri 9.30am–4.30pm, Sat 9.30am–12.30pm. Admission charge. **The Dublin Experience**, a multi-media interpretation of the city, open late May to early Oct, daily 10am–5pm.

**Tyrone House** Not open.

## OUTSIDE DUBLIN

**Avondale House** Rathdrum, Co Wicklow ☎0404 46111. Open May–Oct 11am–5.30pm. Admission charge.

**Castletown House** Cellbridge, Co Kildare ☎6288252. Open Apr–Sep, Mon–Fri 10am–6pm; Sat 11am–6pm; Sun & BH 2–6pm; Oct–Mar, Sun 2–5pm. Admission charge.

**Malahide Castle** (See *Art Galleries*)

**Newbridge House and Park** Donabate, Co Dublin ☎436534. Open Apr–Oct, Tue–Fri 10am–6pm, Sat 11am–6pm, Sun, BH 2–6pm; Nov–Mar, Sun, BH 2–5pm. Special opening for groups of 20 or more. Admission charge. Bus from Eden Quay; trains from Connolly Station with half-hour walk.

**Russborough House** Blessington, Co Wicklow ☎045 65239. Open Easter–31 Oct, Sun, BH 2–5.30pm; and daily in Jul & Aug, 2–5.30pm. Admission charge.

## LIBRARIES

**Central Catholic Library** 74 Merrion Sq South, 2 ☎761264. Nearly 60,000 books and an unusual and comprehensive collection of Irish and foreign Catholic periodicals and newspapers, contemporary and retrospective. Open Mon–Sat 11am–7pm. Closed Sun. Free admission to the reference library.

**The Chester Beatty Library and Gallery of Oriental Art** (see under *Art Galleries*)

**Dublin Public Libraries** Central Library, Ilac Centre, Henry St, 2 ☎734333. A wide range of services includes computer loan-recording, language learning centre, video-viewing, information services, micro-computer use, lending library, children's library, music and record library, business information services, newspapers (Irish and foreign, journals and periodicals). Also trade and telephone directories from around the world. Open Mon–Thu 10am–8pm; Fri–Sat 10am–5pm. Membership and services free of charge; small registration fee to join the record lending section.

**Dublin Public Libraries** Administrative Headquarters, Cumberland House, Fenian St, 2 ☎619000 for information on other services.

**Goethe-Institut** (German Cultural Institute) 37 Merion Sq, 2 ☎611155. Cultural programmes; language courses and library. Open Mon, Tue, Thu 4–8pm; Wed & Fri 10am–6pm; Sat 10am–1pm.

**King's Inns Library** Henrietta St, 1 ☎747134. Admission to members of Inns; others by special permission only. Hours vary during Academic year so phone in advance to check. Open Mon 2–6pm; Tue–Fri 11am–6pm; Sat 10am–1pm.

**The National Library of Ireland** Kildare St, 2 ☎618811. Open Mon 10am–9pm, Tue & Wed 2–9pm, Thu–Fri 10am–5pm, Sat 10am–1pm.

**Marsh's Library** St Patrick's Close, 8 ☎543511. Open Mon–Fri (except Tue) 10am–12.45pm, 2–5pm; Sat 10.30am–12.45pm.

**Royal Dublin Society Library** Ballsbridge, 4 ☎680645. Admission to members and researchers only. Open Tue & Fri 10am–5pm, Wed & Thu 10am–7pm, Sat 11am–5pm. Closed Mon.

**Royal Irish Academy Library** Dawson St, 2 ☎764222. Houses one of the most extensive collections of ancient Irish MSS in the country, including *The Book of the Dun Cow* — history and romances of pre-Christian and Christian periods written on ancient vellum. Open Mon–Fri 10.30am–5.30pm.

**Trinity College Library** (see *Historic Buildings*)

**University College Libraries** Belfield, Earlsfort Ter and Shelbourne Rd ☎693244. Open Mon–Fri 10am–10pm, Sat 9am–1pm. Hours vary during vacations.

## MUSEUMS

**Civic Museum** 58 South William St, 2 ☎794260. Open Tue–Sat 10am–6pm, Sun 11am–2pm.

**Dublin Writers Museum** 18/19 Parnell Sq, 1 ☎722077. Open Mon–Sat 10am–5pm, Sun, BH 2–6pm.

**Guinness Hop Store** Crane St, 8 ☎536700. Sample a glass of Dublin's finest and take a look at Ireland's first brewing museum, with a cooperage display and transport gallery. Beautifully restored sampling area, ideal for relaxing. Open Mon–Fri 10am–3pm.

**Heraldic Museum** Kildare St ☎618811. Open Mon–Fri 10am–12.45pm, 2–4.30pm.

**Irish–Jewish Museum** 3/4 Walworth Rd, 8 ☎534754. Irish–Jewish memorabilia, documents, photographs etc. Open Apr–Sep, Tue, Thur & Sun 11am–3pm; Oct–Apr Sun 10.30am–2.30pm. Bus: 15A/B, 47/47B.

**Museum of Childhood** The Palms, 20 Palmerston Pk, Rathmines, 6 ☎973223. Open Jul & Aug, Tue–Sun 2–5.30pm; Sep, Nov–Jun, Sun

2–5.30pm. Closed Oct. Admission charge.

**The National Museum** Kildare St, 2 ☎618811. Open Tue–Sat 10am–5pm, Sun 2–5pm.

**National Wax Museum** Granby Row, 1 ☎726340. Not a national institution in spite of its name. Life-size figures of Irish people of historical, political, acting and sporting note. Chamber of Horrors. Open Mon–Sat 10am–5.30pm, Sun 1–5.30pm. Admission charge.

**Natural History Museum** Merrion St, 2 ☎618811. Open Tue–Sat 10am–5pm, Sun 2–5pm.

**Pearse Museum** St Enda's Pk, Rathfarnham, 14 ☎934208. The family home of patriot Padraic Pearse and his brother Willie, where they later founded an Irish boys' school; documented in a 20-minute audio-visual show. Open May–Aug 10am–12.30pm & 2–6pm; Mar, Apr, Sep & Oct until 5.30pm, Jan & Dec until 3.30pm, Feb & Nov until 4.30pm.

**RTE Broadcasting Museum** 27 Lr Rathmines Rd, Portobello, 6 ☎932798. Early wireless and TV receivers, phonographs, musical boxes, etc laid out in part of a church. Open mornings by appointment. Bus: 15.

## OUTSIDE DUBLIN

**Howth Transport Museum** Howth Castle, Howth, Co Dublin ☎475623/480831. Fire engines, lorries, trucks, tractors, including the celebrated Hill of Howth No 9 Tram. Open Sat, Sun & BHs 2–6pm. Admission charge.

**James Joyce Museum** James Joyce Tower, Sandycove, Dun Laoghaire, Co Dublin ☎2809265. Open Apr–Oct, Mon–Sat 10–5pm (closed 1–2pm), Sun 2.30–6pm. Admission charge.

**National Maritime Museum** Haigh Ter, Dun Laoghaire, Co Dublin ☎2800969. Open 1 May–Sep, 2.30–5.30pm every day except Mon (open BH). Admission charge.

**National Stud** Tully, Co Kildare. Open Easter–October Mon–Fri 10am–5pm, Sat 10am–6pm, Sun 2–6pm.

## OBSERVATORY

**Dunsink Observatory** Dunsink, Co Dublin ☎387911/387959. Dunsink is one of the oldest observatories in the world and includes a 12in refractor, in the South Telescope, built by Grubb's of Dublin in 1863, which is used on Open Nights if the sky is clear. Exhibits. Open Sep–Mar, 1st & 3rd Sat 8–10pm. Admission free but tickets must be obtained in advance by sending a sae to the Secretary.

## PARKS & GARDENS

**National Botanic Garden** Glasnevin, 9. Open Mon–Sat 9am–6pm, Sun 11am–6pm in summer; Mon–Sat 10am–4.30pm in winter.

**Phoenix Park** 7. Open daily.

**St Enda's Park** Rathfarnham, 14. Twenty-five acres of parkland up against the Dublin Mountains; a leaflet from the Pearse museum will guide you along the Wayfarer nature trail. Open 10am–dusk. Bus: 16, 47B.

**St Stephen's Green** 2. Open Mon–Sat 8am to dusk, Sun 10am–dusk.

## OUTSIDE DUBLIN

**Fernhill Gardens** ☎956000. Open Mar–Nov Tue–Sat, BH, 11am–5pm, Sun 2–6pm.

**Howth Castle** Howth, Co Dublin. Grounds open daily all year, 8am–sunset. Admission charge.

**Japanese Gardens** Tully, Co Kildare ☎045 21251. Open Etr–Oct, Mon–Fri 10am–5pm, Sat & BH, 10am–6pm, Sun 2–6pm. Admission charge.

**Kilruddery** ☎863405. Open May, June & Sep 1–5pm.

**Mount Usher Gardens** Ashford ☎0404 40116. Open 17 Mar–31 Oct Mon–Fri 10.30am–5.30pm, Sun 11am–6pm. Admission charge.

**Powerscourt Demesne**
Enniskerry, Co Wicklow
☎867676. Open Mar–Oct
9.30am–5.30pm; Waterfall, all
year 10.30am–7pm (dusk in
winter).

**St Anne's Park** Mount
Prospect Ave, Clontarf, Co
Dublin. Avenues of trees,
playing pitches, woodland, a
rose garden, bridges,
archways and a lake. Open
daily. Bus: 30 or 44A, or take
the Dart to Killester.

### ZOO

**Zoological Gardens** Phoenix
Park, 7 ☎771425, Open all
year Mon–Sat 9.30am–6pm.
Sun from 11am. Admission
charge. This is one of
Europe's oldest zoos.

# Entertainment

Nightclubs, with few
exceptions, double as discos
and are basically extensions
of pub life which closes
down by law at 11.30pm
(11pm in winter). Drinks may
be expensive. Visiting
cabaret artistes are rare but
Dublin gets more than its fair
share of visiting top-class
rock groups and singers on
the world circuit. The
massive Point Depot at
North Wall is the main
venue for major concerts.

The National Concert Hall
provides a magnificent
setting not only for home
and visiting classical
musicians, but also for folk,
jazz, dance and many other
forms of entertainment.

Dublin has a wide
selection of first-class
cinemas and a pub culture
that needs no elaboration
except to specify those that
feature Irish traditional music
and ballads on a regular
basis.

What most visitors find
astounding however (and
something which Dubliners
tend to take for granted) is
the sheer diversity and
quality of Irish theatre. Each
theatre has its own identity,
but the one any tourist will
probably want to see is the
Abbey — the Irish National
Theatre.

October sees the annual
celebration of the Dublin
Theatre Festival, a two-
sometimes three-week
packed programme that
attracts a dynamic array of
international companies and,
in the best tradition, goes on
against awesome financial
odds.

Programmes of events for
the major venues are usually
available from tourist offices
and department stores such

as Switzers and Brown
Thomas; the National
Concert Hall publishes a
monthly calendar of events.
Best source of information
on every activity going on in
the city is *In Dublin*
magazine, a fortnightly
publication that comes out
on Thursdays; or see the
evening newspapers.

### CABARET

Some of these are dinner
shows; some give an option.
Check when booking.

**Abbey Tavern** Howth, Co
Dublin ☎390282

**Braemor Rooms** Country
Club, Churchtown, 14
☎988664/981016/982308

**Clontarf Castle** Castle
Avenue, 3 ☎332321

**Doyle's Irish Cabaret**
Burlington Hotel, Upr Leeson
St, 4 ☎605222.
(May–October)

**Embankment City** Saggart,
Co Dublin ☎512032

**Jurys Irish Cabaret** Jurys
Hotel, Ballsbridge, 4 ☎605000.
(May–October, 6 nights a
week)

**Mother Redcap's Tavern** Back
Lane, 8 ☎533960

### CINEMAS

**Adelphi** Mid Abbey St, 1
☎730433

**Carlton** Upr O'Connell St, 1
☎731609

**Classic** Harolds Cross Rd, 6
☎975324

**Light House** Middle Abbey
St, 1 ☎730438

**Savoy** Upr O'Connell St, 1
☎748487

**Screen** College St, 2
☎714988

**Screen** O'Connell Bridge, 1
☎746000

**Spanish Film Club** Spanish
Cultural Institute, 58
Northumberland Rd, 4
☎682024

### CONCERT HALLS

Classical music recitals are
also held in churches and
halls around the city.

**The National Concert Hall**
Earlsfort Ter, 2 ☎711888;
711533 (credit card
bookings). An Events Listing
for the Concert Hall is
available each month from
the NCH itself, Tourist
Offices and other outlets.

**Point Depot** East Link Bridge
☎363633/366777

**RDS** Ballsbridge, 4 ☎680645

### DISCOS/NIGHTCLUBS

In a city where nightclubs
open with a flourish and die
with a whimper, to try listing
them all would be foolish.
The following is just a
sample of those which
appear to be there to stay.

**Annabel's** Burlington Hotel, 4
☎605222. (Full licence)

**Dungeon's** Fitzpatrick Castle
Killiney ☎840700

**Lily Langtry's** 45 Nassau St, 2
☎6797539

**McGonagles** 21a St Anne St,
2 ☎774402

**The Night Train** O'Dwyers,
Lr Mount St, 2 ☎761717

**Pink Elephant** South
Frederick St, 1 ☎775876

**Strings** Lr Leeson, 2 ☎613664

**Suesey Street** 25a Lr Leeson
St, 2 ☎686674

**Tamango's** Sands Hotel, Portmarnock, Co Dublin ☎460003/460107

**Waterfront** 14/15 Sir John Rogerson Quay, 2 ☎778466

## JAZZ

Jazz in Dublin takes the form of regular weekly sessions in pubs and hotels around the city. Some have a cover charge so be prepared, or ask first. For details check *In Dublin* magazine or evening newspapers.

## OPERA

DGOS Opera Ireland annually presents two seasons of opera at the Gaiety Theatre. Opera Theatre Company specialises in innovative, small scale productions designed to tour. Visiting opera companies regularly appear at **The RDS** and **The Point**. DGOS Opera Ireland, S Circular Rd, 8 ☎535519; Opera Theatre Company, 18 Kildare St, 2 ☎614884.

## ROCK

Major rock concerts in Dublin usually take place at **The Point**, **The RDS**, Ballsbridge, 4 and **The National Stadium**, South Circular Rd, 8. For concert

information and/or tickets, see Concert Tickets under *Shopping* (below).

There are also a number of venues around the city noted for nurturing up-and-coming, as well as established, rock talent; the Baggot Inn, 143 Lr Baggot St (☎761430) is one of them. For others, see *In Dublin*.

## THEATRES

**Abbey and Peacock Theatres** Lower Abbey St, 2 ☎787222. Irish national theatre.

**Andrew's Lane Theatre & Studio** ☎679 5720

**Dublin Theatre Festival** 47 Nassau St, 2 ☎778439

**Dublin University Players** 4 Trinity College, 2 ☎774673

**Focus Theatre** 6 Pembroke Place, 2 ☎763071

**Gaiety Theatre** Sth King St, 2 ☎771717

**Gate Theatre** 1 Cavendish Row, 1 ☎733210

**Lambert Puppet Theatre** Clifton Lane, Monkstown, Co Dublin ☎2800974

**Olympia Theatre** Dame St, 2 ☎777744

**Project Arts Centre** 39 East Essex St, 2 ☎712321 Interesting experimental work.

**Tivoli** Francis St ☎535998

## TRADITIONAL MUSIC

Several pubs around the city have traditional nights, either organised or impromptu. A selection is given below; full details from *In Dublin* and evening newspapers.

**Comhaltas Ceoltóirí Éireann** 32 Belgrave Sq, Monkstown, Co Dublin ☎800295. Central source of information; céilis and music session several nights a week.

**An Béal Bocht** 58 Charlemont St, 2 ☎755614

**The Culturlann** 32 Belgrave Sq, Monkstown, Co Dublin ☎800295

**The Brazen Head** Lr Bridge St, 8 ☎6795186

**Hughes's** Chancery St, 7 ☎726540

**Kitty O'Shea's** 23 Upr Canal St, 4 ☎609965

**O'Donoghue's** Merrion Row, 2 ☎614303

**The Merchant** 12 Bridge St, 8 (off Merchant's Quay) ☎793797

**Purty Kitchen** Dun Laoghaire, Co Dublin ☎801257

**Slattery's** 129 Capel St, 2 ☎740416

# Shopping

South of the river (and of O'Connell Bridge) has always been considered the fashionable end of Dublin, with Grafton Street at its heart; the north side, for the more budget-conscious, includes the city's main thoroughfare, O'Connell Street. Just off O'Connell Street lies Henry Street, one of the busiest and most lucrative retailing streets in Europe and focal point for north-side shoppers. The O'Connell/Henry Street area has department stores.

Lying within these shopping districts are a number of comparatively young shopping complexes. South of the river, the

Powerscourt Townhouse Centre on Clarendon Street is an aesthetically pleasing, bright, relaxing, shopping complex, converted from a 200-year-old mansion and courtyard. Its Crafts and Antiques Gallery in particular is worth a long browse and the centre is a popular rendezvous.

The Royal Hibernian Way, built on the site of the lamented Hibernian Hotel on Dawson Street, has become Dublin's newest showcase for designers of glamour, elegance and wealth.

The Tower Design Craft Centre is part of the industrial Development Authority's imaginative

programme for industrial renewal and job creation in Dublin's inner city. Once a sugar refinery, the Tower now houses more than 35 workshops. In Rathfarnham, the Marlay Craft Courtyard is a similar enterprise, converted from a 200-year-old courtyard building, and can form the basis of a lovely day out at the foot of the Dublin Mountains.

The Ilac Centre (pronounced eye-lack) has Dunnes Stores — Ireland's largest, cheapest chain store, where T-shirts and tights, pure wool sweaters and suits can be bought at bargain-basement prices.

For design, finish and

value, check out middle- to up-market clothing by Irish designers in Irish linen, tweeds and wool. The work of young and talented contemporary artists may be seen and bought at bargain prices in art galleries around the city, and in the crafts category, handmade pottery and jewellery are excellent buys. Waterford Crystal prices will be the same whichever shop you choose, so shop around for choice rather than value. (Switzers' Waterford Crystal Palace stocks the entire range.) There are other brands of Irish crystal available however, and it may be worth your while comparing prices for similar pieces.

Where Dublin really excels is in the individuality and proliferation of its gifted craftworkers, whose work (for now) is selling at only a fraction of its worth.

## ANTIQUES

Antique shops around Dublin tend to be found in clusters; the following are good areas to try:

The Antique Gallery, Powerscourt Townhouse Centre; Bachelor's Walk, Clarendon St, Dawson St, Duke St, Francis St, Kildare St, Molesworth St, Ormond Quay, South Anne St.

Fine Arts, Antique and Furniture sales are held in various sale rooms in the city at regular intervals. The Fine Arts section in Saturday's *Irish Times* is a good source of up-to-date information.

## BOOKSELLERS

**The Bookshop** Rathfarnam Shopping Centre, 14 ☎934733

**Books Unlimited** Northside Shopping Centre, Coolock, 5 ☎480066; Unit 46 Donaghmede Shopping Centre, 13 ☎470952; 70 Talbot St, 1 ☎742945

**Books Upstairs** College Green, 2 ☎6796687

**Cathach Books** 10 Duke St, 2 ☎718676

**Easons** 40 Lr O'Connell St, 1 ☎733811

**Dublin Book Shop** 24 Grafton St, 2 ☎775568

**Greene & Co** 16 Clare St, 2 ☎762554. New and secondhand books.

**Fred Hanna Ltd** 27/29 Nassau St, 2 ☎771255

**Hodges Figgis** 41 Dawson St, 2 ☎774754

**The Library Shop** Trinity College, College St, 2 ☎772941. Maps, atlases and travel books.

**The Paperback Centre** 14 Stillorgan ☎886341

**Waterstones Bookshop** 7 Dawson St, 2 ☎6791415

**George Webb** 5 Crampton Quay, 1 ☎777489. Trays of book bargains outside, inside Victorian plate-books, old books of Irish interest.

## CONCERT TICKETS

**HMV** 18 Henry St, 1 ☎732899. 65 Grafton St, 2 ☎795332. ☎795364 (24 hrs) for credit card bookings.

**Golden Discs** (see *Records & Cassettes*)

**McCullough Piggott** Suffolk St, 2 ☎773138

## CRAFTS

**Crafts Council of Ireland** Powerscourt Townhouse ☎6797383

**Best of Irish** 5 Nassau St, 2 ☎6799117

**The Craft Gallery** Powerscourt Townhouse Centre, 2 ☎6799233

**Dublin Crystal Glass Co.** Carysfort Ave, Blackrock, Co Dublin ☎2887932

**Gaelic Design** Temple Bar, 2 ☎711146

**The Kilkenny Shop** Nassau St, 2 ☎777066

**Marlay Craft Courtyard** Marlay Park, Rathfarnham, 16 ☎942083. 200-year-old courtyard divided into workshops leased to professional craftworkers.

**Needlecraft** 27 Dawson St, 2 ☎772493. Wools, art, needlework and tapestries.

**O'Farrell Workshops Ltd** 62 Dawson St, 2 ☎770862

**This is It** U13 Irish Life Mall, Talbot St, 1 ☎728551

**Tower Design Craft Centre** Pearse St, 2 ☎775655. Similar to Marlay Park.

## DELICATESSENS

**John Caviston** 59 Glasthule Rd, Sandycove, Co Dublin ☎2809120

**Cornucopia** Wicklow St, 2 ☎777583

**\*Dunn's** 6 Upper Baggot St, 2 ☎602688

**Fitzpatricks** 41 Lr Camden St, 2 ☎753996

**Fothergills** 141 Upper Rathmines Rd, 6 ☎962511

**Gourmet Shop** 48 Highfield Rd, 6 ☎970365

**Magills** 14 Clarendon St, 2 ☎713830

**\*McConnell** 38 Grafton St, 2 ☎774344

*\*Denotes those which stock and mail smoked salmon to Britain, USA and mainland Europe.*

## DEPARTMENT STORES

**Arnott & Co** 12 Henry St, 1 ☎721111

**BHS (Dublin) Ltd** O'Connell St, 1 ☎720466

**Brown Thomas & Co** 15 Grafton St, 2 ☎6795666

**Clery & Co** O'Connell St, 1 ☎786000

**Dunnes Stores Ltd** Ilac Centre, 1 ☎730211; St Stephen's Gn ☎751111

**The Kilkenny Shop** Nassau St, 2 ☎777066

**Marks & Spencer** 24 Mary St, 1 ☎728833; 28 Grafton St, 2 ☎6797855

**Primark** 47 Mary St, 1 ☎727788

**Roches' Stores** 54 Henry St, 1 ☎730044

**Switzer & Co** 92 Grafton St, 2 ☎776821

## FASHION ACCESSORIES

**H Johnston Ltd** 11 Wicklow St, 2 ☎771249

**Kamouflage Ltd** 50 Dawson St, 2 ☎777696

**Ciaran Peters** Parnell Mall, Ilac Centre, Henry St, 1 ☎729412

## FASHION-DESIGNERS

The Design Centre at Powerscourt features a wide range of Ireland's leading designers, including **Tony Close, Mary Gregory, Sharon Keogh, Louise Kennedy, Lainey Keogh** and **Mariad Whisker.**

Other designers include: **Paul Costelloe** Brown Thomas, Grafton St ☎6795666

**Pat Crowley** 14 Duke St, 2 ☎710219

**Ibi Jorgensen** 11 Harcourt St, 2 ☎758813

**Michael Mortell** Westbury Centre ☎791600

**Quin & Donnelly** Branches of A-Wear

**John Rocha** Chinatown, Brown Thomas & branches of A-Wear

**Thomas Wolfangel** 158 Pembroke Rd, 4 ☎604069

## FASHION-WOMEN

**Richard Alan & Co** 58 Grafton St, 2 ☎775149; Clarendon St, 2 ☎710320

**A-Wear** 26 Grafton St, 2 ☎717200

**Austin Reed** 51 Dawson St, 2 ☎6795884

**Aquascutum** 51c Dawson St, 2 ☎770522

**Laura Ashley** 60 Grafton St, 2 ☎795433

**Pia Bang** Grafton St, 2 ☎715065

**Benetton** 81 Grafton St, 2 ☎779877

**Ebony** 71 Grafton St, 2 ☎774655

**Firenze** Westbury Centre, 2 ☎6791600

**Monica John** William Elliot

Centre, Wicklow St, 2 ☎794290

**Koko Bleu** Royal Hibernian Way, 2 ☎715079

**Otokio** 3 South Anne St, 2 ☎777325

**Sortez** Westbury Centre, 2 ☎6799048

**Specials** 80 Grafton St. 2 ☎774499

**Jenny Vander** Antique Clothing, 20 South City Market, off South Gt George's St, 2 ☎770406

## FASHION-MEN

**Alias Tom** 2 Duke Lane, 2 ☎715443

**Michael Barrie** 20 Duke St, 2 ☎715265

**Louis Copeland** 30 Lr Pembroke St, 2 ☎610110; 19 Wicklow St ☎777038

**Ecru High Fashion** 31 Grafton St, 2 ☎774133

**F X Kelly** 48 Grafton St, 2 ☎778211

**Kennedy & McSharry** 39 Nassau St, 2 ☎778770

**Kevin & Howlin Ltd** 31 Nassau St, 2 ☎770257

**Savoy Taylors Guild** 47 Grafton St, 2 ☎713660

**John Taylor Ltd** 35 Kildare St, 2 ☎616007; 34 Baggot St, 2 ☎600522

## FISHING TACKLE

**ABC Angling** 15 St Mary's Abbey, 7 ☎731525

**Rory's Fishing Tackle** 17a Temple Bar, 2 ☎772351. Sole agents for Bruce and Walker.

## FOOTWEAR

Shoeshops have virtually taken over Grafton St and a good deal of Henry St. The following are shops that stock high-fashion or unusual footwear:

**Ecco** 26 Wicklow St, 2 ☎6798714; 50 Dawson St, 2 ☎777696

**Natural Shoe Store** 25 Drury St, 2 ☎714978

**Thomas Patrick** 77 Grafton St, 2 ☎713866. Bruno Magli Shop upstairs.

**Carl Scarpa** 25 Grafton St, 2 ☎777846

**The Shoe Boutique** 22 Wicklow St, 2 ☎777491

## FURNITURE

**O'Hagen Design** 99 Capel St, 1 ☎726440

## HERALDRY

**Heraldic Artists Ltd** 3 Nassau St, 2 ☎6797020

**Heraldic House** 36 Upr O'Connell St, 1 ☎741133

**Thomas and Emmet O'Baoill** Tower Design Craft Centre, Pearse St, 2 ☎775655

## JEWELLERS

**Patrick Flood** Goldsmith Designer, Powerscourt Townhouse Centre, 2 ☎6794256

**Emma Stewart Liberty** Powerscourt Townhouse Centre, 2 ☎6791603

**Tower Design Craft Centre** Pearse St, 2 ☎775655

**Weir & Sons** 96 Grafton St, 2 ☎779678

**West** 33 Grafton St, 2 ☎777275

## LINGERIE

**Susan Hunter** 13 Westbury Centre, 2 ☎791271

## MARKETS

**Blackrock Market** Sat 11am–5.30pm, Sun 12am–5.30pm.

**Christ Church Market** 8. Fri, Sat, Sun, 10.30am–5.30pm.

**Dublin Corporation Market** St Michan's St, 7. Fruit, fish, vegetables and flowers. Mon–Fri 7am–5pm; Tue 7am–4pm; Sat 7.30am–11am.

**Iveagh Market** Francis St, 8 Tue–Sat 9am–6pm.

**Liberty Market** Meath St, 8. Clothes and household goods. Fri and Sat.

**Moore Street Market** 1 Fruit, flowers and vegetables, just off Henry St. Mon–Sat 9am–6pm.

## MILLINERS

**Kamouflage** 50 Dawson St, 2 ☎777696

**Paul Moreland** Powerscourt Townhouse Centre, 2 ✆793832

### RECORDS AND CASSETTES

**Claddagh Records** 2 Cecilia St, 2 ✆770262. Specialist folk.

**Dolphin Discs** Branches in Moore St, 1; Capel St, 1; Marlboro St, 1; Talbot St, 1 ✆729998

**Golden Disc Group** Branches at 1 Grafton Arcade, 2; 8 North Earl St, 1; Ilac Centre, 1; 17 Upr Liffey St, 1 ✆6792118

**HMV** Branches at 65 Grafton St, 2 ✆795332 and 18 Henry St, 1 ✆732899

**International Record Lending Library** 17a South

Anne St, 2 ✆770327

**McCullough Piggott Ltd** 11 Suffolk St, 2 ✆773138

**Music Maker** 4 St Mary's Abbey, 1 ✆730533; 29 Exchequer St ✆779004

**Virgin Megastore** Aston Quay, 2 ✆777361

**Walton's Musical Galleries** 2 Nth Frederick St, 1 ✆747805

### SPORTS GOODS

**Arnott & Co** Henry St, 1 ✆721111

**Elvery's** Suffolk St, 2 ✆776744

**Great Outdoors Ltd** Chatham Hse, Chatham St, 2 ✆6794293

**Marathon Sports** Ilac Centre,

1 ✆728868; 40 Grafton St, 2 ✆6795794

**Scout Shop** 14 Fownes St, 2 ✆712055

### WOOLLENS

**Blarney Woollen Mills** 21/23 Nassau St, 2 ✆710068

**Cleo Ltd** 18 Kildare St, 2 ✆761421

**Dublin Woollen Co** Metal Bridge Corner, 1 ✆770301

**The Irish Scene** Powerscourt Townhouse Centre, 2 ✆794061

**Monaghan's** Grafton Arcade, Grafton St, 2 ✆770823

**The Sweater Shop** 9 Wicklow St, 2 ✆713270

# Sports

Up-to-date information on competition and matches is available in the daily papers, most of which feature comprehensive sports diaries at the weekends. Or consult *In Dublin* magazine.

### ANGLING

For coarse anglers, Dublin's two canals provide good fishing stretches not far from the city. Year-round fishing is possible as there is no legal closed season, but there are 'best' times for different species and visitors are asked to note the conservation laws regarding some. The position regarding licences is under review, at present none is required, nor are permits — except very rarely on private fisheries. If bringing your own bait into Ireland, take care that it is not packed in soil or vegetable material, the importation of which is prohibited by law. Competition details are available in *Ireland Freshwater Angling* and *Gala Angling Festivals* — both available from Irish Tourist offices.

Game anglers need a licence for both salmon and sea trout fishing, though only

one is needed for both. Licences are available from the Central Fisheries Board, Balnagowan House, Mobhi Boreen, Glasnevin (✆379206), the relevant Regional Fisheries Board (see Bord Fáilte sheets below) and from selected tackle dealers. Some salmon fishing is free or available at a nominal charge, but almost all sea trout fisheries are under private or club control. Check with the Fisheries Board.

Sea angling is an all-year-round sport offering huge variety, depending on the time of year. Recommended centres around Dublin include Skerries, Howth and Dun Laoghaire. Anglers are asked to return as many fish as possible alive to the water. The Bord Fáilte booklet *Sea Angling in Ireland* gives details of boats, maps, festivals and bait, and is available from any Irish Tourist Board Literature Depot, PO Box 1083, Dublin 8 (*tel* 747733 for price information). See Bord Fáilte *Information Sheets Nos 10a, 10b, 10c.*

**Irish Federation of Sea Anglers**: Mr Hugh O'Rorke, Secretary, 67 Windsor Drive,

Monkstown, Co Dublin ✆2806873

**Irish Match Angling and Surfcasting Association** (IMASA) Mr Michael Dixon, 36 Ralahine, Ballybrack, Co Dublin ✆854159

### BADMINTON

**Badminton Hall** Whitehall Rd, 12 ✆508101 (office hours) 505966 (court bookings)

**The Badminton Clinic** 64 Ailesbury Grove, 16 ✆980349 for coaching sessions.

### BALLOONING

**Dublin Ballooning Club** 5 Old Bawn, Tallaght ✆517184

### BEACHES

Popular sandy beaches may be found at Dollymount (3½ miles from Dublin), Howth (9 miles), Sutton (7 miles), Portmarnock (9 miles), Donabate (13 miles), Malahide (9 miles), Sandycove (9 miles). Lovely strands for walking and sunbathing close to the south city centre are at Sandymount and Merrion.

### BICYCLE HIRE

**Charleys** 35 Ballylough Rd, 3 ✆744090

**Joe Daly** Lr Main St, Dundrum, 14 ☎981485

**E R Harris** 87c Green Park Rd ☎863357

**Rent-a-bike** 58 Lr Gardiner St, 1 ☎7255399

## BOARDSAILING

Boardsailing is gaining in popularity all the time, and although the Atlantic swells on Ireland's west coast are hard to beat, Dublin will still provide a reasonable challenge for enthusiasts, whatever their experience. See *Bord Fáilte Information Sheet No 28a.*

**Association for Adventure Sports** House of Sport, Longmile Rd, 12 ☎509845

**Irish Boardsailing Association** or **Irish Windsurfing Class Association BIC Sport**, Santry Ave, 9 ☎426577.

**Skerries Boardsailng School** 7 Convent Lane, Skerries, Co Dublin ☎491734/490068 after 6.30pm.

**Fingall Sailing School** Upper Strand, Broadmeadow Estuary, Malahide, Co Dublin ☎451979

**Glenans Irish Sailing Centre** 28 Merrion Sq, Dublin 2 ☎767775/611481

**Wind & Wave Windsurfing of Salthill** Dun Laoghaire ☎2844177

## BOWLING

There are a dozen or so clubs dotted all around the city. For information contact Mr J J Burke, Dookinelly, 13 Glenabbey Rd, Mount Merrion, Co Dublin ☎880255

## BOWLING, TEN PIN

**Crumlin Super Bowl** Crumlin Road, 12 ☎559659

**Dundrum Bowl** Ballinteer Rd, 14 ☎980209

**Stillorgan Bowling Centre** ☎2881656

**The Strand Bowl** 149 Strand Rd, 3 ☎741868

**Tallaght Sportsbowl** Old Bawn, Tallaght ☎599411

## CANOEING

The Liffey Descent (the Irish International Marathon Canoe-Racing Championships) is held in September when 30 million tons of water are released from a reservoir into the River Liffey, turning it from a well-behaved old lady into a raging torrent. See also *Bord Fáilte Information Sheet No 28b.*

**Irish Canoe Union** House of Sport ☎509845

**Irish Canoe Hire** Lackenash, Barnhill Rd, Dalkey, Co Dublin ☎854933/844288

## DIVING

**Irish Underwater Council** National Maritime Museum, Haigh Terrace, Dun Laoghaire ☎800969

**Great Outdoors Diving School** ☎6794293

**Oceantec Adventures** 10 Marine Tce, Dun Laoghaire ☎8010983

## GAELIC GAMES

Gaelic football and hurling are the great rural pastimes on Sunday afternoons in Ireland. Every parish has its club, some traditionally stronger than others, but inter-parish rivalry will always ensure wild enthusiasm, stunning vigour (sometimes literally), and often flashes of real brilliance.

Important matches are the All-Ireland Finals, both played in September. The National League Finals are held in May.

The Gaelic Athletic Association (GAA) is the governing body for Gaelic games in Ireland and its headquarters are in Croke Park where most important matches are played.

**Gaelic Athletic Association** Croke Park, 3 ☎363222. Croke Park has two stands, both considered good (if you can get tickets for them). Of the terraced areas, Hill 16 is packed with atmosphere — but can be turbulent.

## GOLF

*The Golfers' Guide to Ireland* is widely available and gives details helpful to visitors. Bord Fáilte produces a brochure *Only the Best* which features the country's finest courses.

Clubs are accessible and courses are often natural beauty spots. Green fees in Ireland are usually charged on a per day rather than per round basis; they average about £10 per day, but can go as high as £45 for some of the top championship courses. Availability of caddies (without prior arrangement) or golf cars is negligible so visitors are advised to bring only a light 'Sunday' bag as they will probably have to carry it themselves.

**Golfing Union of Ireland** 81 Eglinton Road, 4 ☎269411

**Senior Marketing Executive — Golf** Bord Fáilte, Baggot St Bridge, 2 ☎765871

## GYMS AND EXERCISE CENTRES

**Fitness Studio** Swanville Pl. Lr Rathmines Rd, 6 ☎960967

**Litton Lane Dance Studios** 2 Litton Lane, 1 ☎728044

**Orwell Club** Orwell Rd, 6 ☎976146

**Pulse** Temple Bar, 2 ☎6799620

**Slender Health Studios** 6 Lr Kilmacud Rd, Stillorgan, Co Dublin ☎2886871

**Squash Ireland Ltd** (see *Squash* for addresses and telephone numbers)

**YMCA** Aungier St, 2 ☎782607

## HILL WALKING AND ROCK CLIMBING

One of the five great roads radiating from Tara in ancient Ireland was the Sli Cualann, the Wicklow Way, so called because it crosses part of the former land of Cuala, now Wicklow. The start of the Wicklow Way is served by Dublin City buses.

It follows sheep tracks, forest firebreaks and old bog roads across miles of beautiful open country; there are magnificent views. Much of it lies above 500m where sudden and drastic weather changes can occur; maps and compasses are advisable, and it is not recommended for solitary rambling.

The strong walker could cover all 126km of the Wicklow Way, but there are several shorter walks for the less energetic or those with only a few hours to spare.

Further information from *Bord Fáilte Information Sheets Nos 26a, 26b, 26d, 26e; The Wicklow Guide* (Bord Fáilte); *The Open Road* and *Walking in Wicklow* by J B Malone.

### HORSE RACING

Racing is one of the great Irish sports. Two top-class tracks lie only a few miles south and north of the city centre — Leopardstown and the Phoenix Park respectively.

Big days in the Irish racing calendar include: the Airlie/Coolmore Irish 2000 Guineas (May); Goffs Irish 1000 Guineas (May); the Budweiser Irish Derby (June) — the most glamorous outing of the year; the Irish Oaks (July); and the Jefferson Smurfit Memorial Irish St Leger (October). These are all held at the Curragh in Co Kildare.

Favourite tracks for National Hunt followers include Leopardstown; Fairyouse, Co Meath (where the Irish Grand National is held on Easter Monday); Punchestown (famous for its three-day Festival meeting in late April); and Navan (feature race the Troytown Chase). All lie within an hour's drive of Dublin.

Racegoers in Ireland can place their bets either with the course bookmakers or with the Tote. The Tote pays according to the official starting price regardless of when the bet is placed. It also offers combination bets and a jackpot.

All the Irish national newspapers carry details of the day's race-meetings and carry results on the following day. Other publications include: *Irish Racing Annual*

(ed Smith and McGinty): published in early December, it reviews the previous 12 months of home and international racing; *Guide to Irish Racing* (ed Wall): published end of March, this gives predictions for the year ahead for Flat and National Hunt racing in Ireland; Bord Fáilte booklet *Equestrian Ireland*.

### The Racing Board
Leopardstown, Foxrock, D18
☎2892888

### HORSE RIDING

Hacking and trekking are offered by many riding schools in easy reach of Dublin. See *Bord Fáilte Information Sheet No 16*.

**Bord nag Capall** Irish Horse Board, Irish Farm Centre, Naas Rd, 12 ☎501166

### ICE SKATING

**Dublin Ice Rink** Dolphin's Barn, 8 ☎534153

**Silver Skate Ice Rink** 376 North Circular Rd, 7 ☎301263

### ROWING

The major regatta in Ireland is the Dublin Metropolitan Regatta, held on a straight, 6-laned, 2000 metre course, as required by FISA for International Regattas. The programme is finalised in November; contact Bord Fáilte or the IARU. Islandbridge, the headquarters of most Dublin rowing clubs, is on a point of the River Liffey ideally suited for the sport. Contact House of Sport, Long Mile Rd, 12 ☎509831. See also *Bord Fáilte Information Sheet No 28c*.

### RUGBY UNION

Lansdowne Road is the headquarters of Irish rugby, and is also the venue for all matches played in the Five Nations Championship, including the Triple Crown. These matches are played during January, February and March, and stand-tickets for

home games can be rare.

Lansdowne Road has 22,000 stand-seats divided between stands on both sides of the pitch. Terracing at both ends is adequate but distinctly uncomfortable if it rains (umbrellas will be discouraged by the more vocal behind you) or if conditions become very crowded.

There is a lively club rugby scene around the city. For details see daily newspapers or contact: Irish Rugby Football Union, 62 Lansdowne Rd, 4 ☎684601

### SAILING

The oldest Yacht Club in the world is Irish — the Royal Cork Yacht Club, which celebrated its 250th anniversary in 1970. Dublin has some venerable clubs of her own, however, including the National Yacht Club, the Royal Irish Yacht Club, the Royal St George Yacht Club and the Dun Laoghaire Motor Yacht Club, all situated in Dun Laoghaire. Howth Harbour also has a lively club, and there are several areas along the coastline where dinghy sailing as well as keelboat sailing are popular.

Yachts or dinghies may be brought into Ireland for a temporary period without liability for tax or duty. Owners of sea-going yachts must apply to the harbour masters of all ports in which they wish to anchor. On arrival at the first port of entry, the flag 'Q' should be shown. Contact should then be made with the Customs and Excise Officer or with a Garda. Irish laws on the importation of cats and dogs are extremely restrictive (except from Britain); a licence must be obtained beforehand from the Dept of Agriculture, Dublin 2. Further information from the Irish Yachting Association, 3 Park Rd, Dun Laoghaire, Co Dublin ☎2800239. A full-time secretariat is available to give further information to visiting yachtsmen. See also *Bord Fáilte Information Sheet Nos 28f, 28g*.

## SOCCER

Soccer in Ireland consists mainly of the League of Ireland and occasional international or representative matches. The Irish RFU's ground at Lansdowne Road is the usual venue for big international soccer matches. Less important competitions take place at Dalymount and Tolka Parks on the north side of the city.

League of Ireland matches are played every Sunday afternoon during the season on various grounds around the city. For details see national newspapers or contact: **The Football Association of Ireland** 80 Merrion Sq South, ☎766864

## SQUASH

**Squash Ireland Ltd** Branches at: Clontarf (☎331656) Dalkey (2801515) Dartry (963910) Phoenix Park (385850). Visitors' fees include full gym facilities, sauna, etc.

## SWIMMING BATHS

There is an admission charge to these pools. Telephone individual pools for opening hours.

**Ballyfermot** Le Fanu Park, 10 ☎266504

**Ballymun** Ballymun Shopping Centre, 10 ☎421368

**Coolock** Coolock Shopping Centre, 5 ☎477743

**Crumlin** Windmill Rd, 12 ☎555792

**Finglas** Mellowes Rd, 11 ☎348005

**Townsend St** Linn Snahma Markievicz, 2 ☎770503

**Rathmines** Williams Park, Rathmines, 6 ☎961275

**Sean McDermott St** 1 ☎720752

## OUTSIDE DUBLIN

**Monkstown Indoor Heated Pool** Monkstown, Co Dublin ☎807100. Admission charge.

**Dun Laoghaire** Open Sea Baths, Rainbow Rapids ☎2841690

## TENNIS

Irish Lawn Tennis Association, 54 Wellington Rd, 4 ☎681841

**Bushy Park** Terenure, 6 ☎900320

**Fitzwilliam** Appian Way, 6 ☎603988

**Herbert Park** Ballsbridge, 4 ☎684364

**St Anne's Estate** Dollymount, 3 ☎313697

## WATER-SKIING

**Irish Water-Ski Association** 7 Upper Beaumont Drive, Ballintemple, Cork ☎(201)292411

**Golden Falls Water-Ski Club** Ballymore Eustace, Co Kildare offers facilities to non-club members. ☎855205

# Transport

Dublin is a small, compact city with most of its attractions lying conveniently within a one-mile radius, and many will tell you that the only way to see it is on foot. Because of its one-way street system and a dearth of good signposting, it is not recommended territory for visiting car drivers. You are therefore advised to find a secure car park, leave the car, and choose between walking, finding a bus or taking a taxi.

## BUSES

Dublin's public bus service is regular and comparatively cheap, crossing city and suburbs from around 6.30am on weekdays (9.30am on Sundays) to 11.30pm. 'An Lar' written on the front of a bus means The Centre.

Information on all public transport services may be obtained by telephoning 302222 (9am–9pm weekdays,

Sundays 10am–7pm). Bus Éireann (the Dublin City Bus Service) also runs day tours both around the city and to outlying areas. They start from Dublin Bus, 59 Upr O'Connell St, 1 ☎720000 (ext 3028). Explorer Tickets, for unlimited bus and rail travel, and family and adult one day bus passes are also available from Dublin Bus.

## SUBURBAN TRAINS

Dart (the Dublin Rapid Transit System) is Iarnród Éireann's high-frequency electric rail service extending from Bray, all around Dublin Bay, up to Howth in the north of the city. Starting at 7am and continuing to midnight, trains run about every 5 minutes: a pleasant way to get an overview of Dublin bay and the suburbs.

## TAXIS

Telephone a taxi (see under 'Taxi-Cab Ranks and Shelters'

in the telephone directory), telephone a taxi company, find a taxi rank (see below) or try hailing a passing cab (almost impossible at peak hours.) Standards vary from cigarette-infested to spotless, (they are improving rapidly). Fares are metered and are subject to a minimum charge within a 10-mile radius of the city centre, plus an extra charge for each passenger, a baggage charge and a night surcharge. Tips run to about 10 per cent. Fares for journeys outside the city centre may be negotiated directly with the driver.

### City taxi ranks

Amiens St, 1; Angle, Ranelagh, 6; Aston's Quay, 1; Burlington Hotel, 4; College Green, 2; Crescent, Malahide Rd, 3; Eccles St, 7; Eden Quay, 1; Lansdowne Rd, 4 (near Jury's Hotel); Marine Rd, Dun Laoghaire; O'Connell St, Upr & Lr, 1;

Rathmines Rd, Upper, 6; St Stephen's Green, 2; Terenure Rd N. 6; Westland Row station, 2; 14a Wexford St, 2

## CAR HIRE

See *Bord Fáilte Information Sheet No 50a* for a list of companies who are members of the Car Rental Council, and operate according to a Code of Standards drawn up by them and Bord Fáilte. They include:

**Avis Rent-a-Car Ltd** 1 Hanover St East, 2 ☎774010; Dublin Airport ☎372369

**Boland's Car Hire Rentals** 38 Pearse St, 2 ☎770704

**Budget** Dublin Airport ☎370919; Dublin City ☎379802

**Hertz Rent-a-Car** Dublin Airport ☎429333; Hotel Conrad ☎766920; Leeson St Up ☎602255

**Murrays Europcar Rent-a-Car** Baggot St Bridge, 4 ☎681777

## CAR PARKS

Visitors are advised to leave their cars in official car-parks. There are over a dozen

controlled and manned car parks around the city centre, including those at: Setanta Place, 2; Drury St, 2; Marlborough St, 1; Ilac Centre, 1.

## HORSE-DRAWN CABS

Restored horse-drawn cabs can be taken from North St Stephen's Green in summer or may be hired (by appointment only) from Paddy Sarsfield, 5 Lr Kevin St, 8 ☎755995, Michael Stanley ☎535490 or James Byrne ☎543153.

# Useful Information

## AUTOMOBILE ASSOCIATION

**AA Centre** 23 Suffolk St, 2 ☎779481. Mon–Fri 9am–5pm, Sat 9am–12.30pm.

**Dublin South** 23 Rock Hill, Blackrock ☎833555

## BANKS

From Monday to Friday most Dublin banks are open from 10am to 3pm (except Thursday when they remain open until 5pm). Closed Saturday, Sunday and Bank Holidays. Dublin Airport Bank is the exception, remaining open every day (except Christmas Day) from 7.30am–11pm; from October to March, 8.30am–9.30pm.

Allied Irish Banks and Bank of Ireland, the two main banking groups in Ireland, have branches all over Dublin; those in the city centre include:

### AIB

64 Grafton St, 2 ☎773584
100 Grafton St, 2 ☎713011
7 Dame St, 2 ☎6793211
10 Lr O'Connell St, 2 ☎730555
63 Upr O'Connell St, 2 ☎731500
Group Headquarters, Bankcentre, Ballsbridge, 4 ☎600311

**Bank of Ireland**
Airport ☎420433

2 College Green, 2 ☎776801
6 Lr O'Connell St, 1 ☎729799
39 St Stephen's Green East, 2 ☎761976
1 Westmoreland St, 1 ☎776801
Group Headquarters, Lr Baggot St, 2 ☎615933

**Bank of America** Russell Court, St Stephen's Green, 2 ☎781222

**Bank of Nova Scotia** 65 St Stepen's Green, 2 ☎781388

**Barclays Bank** 47 St Stephen's Green, 2 ☎611777

**Northern Bank** 27 College Green, 2 (Agents for Midland) ☎6798788

**Ulster Bank Ltd** 33 College Green, 2 (Agents for Nat West) ☎6799199

**Algemene Bank Nederland** 121 St Stephen's Green, 2 ☎717333

**Bank of America** Russell Ct, St Stephen's Green, 2 ☎781222

**Bank of Nova Scotia** Canada House, 65 St Stephen's Green, 2 ☎781388

**Banque Nationale de Paris** 111 St Stephen's Green West, 2 ☎712811

**Chase Bank Ltd** 18 St Stephen's Green North, 2 ☎785111

**TSB** 114 Lr Grafton St ☎6798133

## BUREAUX DE CHANGE

Most banks have facilities for cashing travellers' cheques and exchanging currency. Travellers' cheques are accepted by most hotels, large shops, transport and travel companies. Facilties are also provided by:

**Dublin & East Tourism** 14 Upr O'Connell St, 1 ☎747733

**Thomas Cook** 118 Grafton St, 2 ☎771721/771307

**American Express** 116 Grafton St, 2 ☎772874

## CHEMISTS (Late Night)

**Brady's** 12 Upr Camden St, 2 ☎751531

**Corrigan's** 80 Malahide Rd 3 ☎338803

**Costello's** 25 Marino Mart, 3 ☎338571

**O'Connell's** 6 Henry St, 1 ☎731077; 55 O'Connell St, 1 ☎730427; 310 Harold's X Rd, 6 ☎973977; 85 Terenure Rd N, 6 ☎907179

## DOCTORS AND DENTISTS

For a list of doctors and dentists, see the *Golden Pages* telephone directory.

**Irish Medical Organisation** 10 Fitzwilliam Place, 2 ☎767273

**Irish Dental Association** 16 Fitzwilliam Sq, 5 ☎618358

### ELECTRICITY

200 volts/50 cycles is usual in Ireland. Many hotels have 220/110 volt plugs for shavers.

### EMERGENCIES

In life-threatening emergencies, telephone 999 from any call box and say which service is required — Fire Brigade, Police or Ambulance. There is no charge for the call. See also *Hospitals*.

### GENEALOGY

See *Bord Fáilte Information Sheet No 21, Tracing Your Ancestors*.

**Hibernian Research** Windsor House, 22 Windsor Rd, 6 ☎966522 (24 hours)

**Genealogical Office** Kildare St, 2 ☎618811

### GUIDES

**Dublin & East Tourism** 14 Upr O'Connell St, 2 ☎747733

**Grayline Dublin City Tours** 14 O'Connell St, 2 ☎744466

**Bus Éireann** c/o Dublin & East Tourism, or Central Bus Station (Busaras), 35 Lr Abbey St, 1 or (personal callers only) 59 Upr O'Connell St, 1

**Tour Guides Ireland** 12 Parliament St, 2 ☎6794291

### HEALTH

**Visitors from another EEC country.**
If a visitor to Ireland from another EEC country is eligible under EEC Social Security Regulations (ie if they are insured workers), they and their dependents, if they are on a short visit (eg holidays or a business trip) can receive urgent medical care for sudden sickness or accident in the same way as an Irish national who holds a medical card. For a list of doctors contact Eastern Health Board, Emmet House, 138/140 Thomas St, 8 ☎719222. Hours 9am–5pm Monday–Friday.

It is necessary for visitors from EEC countries other than UK to present Form E111 when visiting a doctor on contract or hospital. Visitors from the UK need only give their UK address and their national insurance number to the doctor on contract from whom they are seeking treatment. Further details from the Chief Executive Officer, Eastern Health Board, 1 James's St, 8 ☎537951 or from local Health Centres.

**Visitors from non-EEC countries**
You can obtain health services as above, but will have to pay (depending on your insurance arrangements).

**Urgent medical treatment**
Emergency medical services are available 24 hours a day. Ring any of the hospitals below to find out which ones are 'on call'. Or telephone 999 for an ambulance.

### HOSPITALS

**Jervis Street Hospital** Jervis St, 1 ☎723355

**Mater Misericordiae** Eccles St, 7 ☎301122

**National Maternity Hospital** Holles St, 2 ☎610277

**Rotunda Maternity Hospital** Parnell Sq, 1 ☎730700

**St James's** James's St, 8 ☎537941

**St Vincent's** Elm Park, 4 ☎2694533

### LOOS

The average Dubliner will not resort to a public convenience if he or she can help it, preferring to find a convenient pub, restaurant or hotel. Pubs are probably the best bet as they don't have doors that demand a 5p piece when you are least likely to have it. Department stores (Arnotts, Clery's, Brown Thomas, Switzers) all have loos but usually have endless queues as well. There is a public convenience in the city centre in the 'triangle' between Trinity College and Westmoreland Street.

### NEWSAGENT/NEWSPAPERS

Daily papers include:

**Irish Independent** Independent House, 90 Middle Abbey St, 1 ☎731666

**Irish Press** Burgh Quay, 2 ☎713333

**Irish Times** D'Olier St, 2 ☎6792022

Foreign newspapers are available from:
**Bus Stop** Gaiety Corner, 52 Grafton St, 2 ☎773661

**Eason & Son** 40/42 Lr O'Connell St, 1 ☎733811

### OPTICIANS

See *Golden Pages* telephone directory. For emergency spectacle repairs:

**Donal McNally Opticians** 75 Grafton Street ☎715499 & branches.

### PHOTOGRAPHY

Most pharmacies sell and develop film. For speedy print developing, one-hour shops around the city include:

**Fujicolor Service Centre** 148 Lr Baggot St, 2 ☎789644

**One Hour Photo** 110 Grafton St, 2 ☎774472

### POST OFFICES

Central post offices such as those at St Andrew St (off Wicklow St) and South Anne St (off Grafton St) are open from 9am–5.30pm on weekdays only. The General Post Office (GPO), O'Connell Street, ☎728888 is open 8am–8pm on weekdays, and on Sundays and Bank Hols from 10.30am–6pm.

### TELEPHONES

Public telephones called 'Payphones' enable a caller to dial local, trunk and international calls direct. Payphones accept 5p, 10p, 20p and 50p coins. The General Post Office, O'Connell St, also has international telephoning facilities. For help with calls, the operator can be reached by dialling 10.

### TELEVISION & RADIO

Radio Telefís Éireann, Donnybrook, Dublin 4, (☎269311) operates the state-run radio and television system. The BBC, British Independents and Channel 4 are also picked up along the east coast together with a number of satellite channels.

**Radio 1** *88.5MHz*
News, shows, light music.

**Radio 2** *90.7 MHz*
Pop music.

**Radio na Gaeltachta** *92.9 MHz*
Irish language channel.

**FM3** *92.9 MHz*
Classical music (afternoons — shared channel).

### TIPPING

Where tips are given, they can be in the order of 10–15 per cent, for instance to taxi drivers, hairdressers, barbers, and waiting staff in hotels and restaurants. Some hotels and restaurants incorporate a service charge in the bill.

Hotel porters expect a tip of around 50p a bag and official car park attendants usually get the same.

### TOURIST INFORMATION

A wealth of local and national information is available from Irish tourist offices dotted all over the country. The knowledge of the staff is backed up by masses of maps, guides, books and leaflets, many of which are free or available at a nominal charge. A Room Reservation Service (for personal callers) will book visitors into Bord Fáilte (Irish Tourist Board) approved premises for a small fee.

**Dublin & East Tourism** 14 Upr O'Connell St, 1 ☎747733 (Open all year round) and Dublin Airport ☎376387 (Open all year round)

**Bord Fáilte** Baggot St, 2 ☎747733/765871. (Open 3 March–October)

### ANNUAL EVENTS IN DUBLIN

**March** Feis Ceoil
St Patrick's Day Parade
Dublin Film Festival

**April** Dublin Grand Opera Society Spring Season
Irish Grand National

**May** Spring Show and Industries Fair

**June** 16th Bloomsday
Dublin Street Carnival

**July** Carrolls Irish Open Golf Championships

**August** Dublin Horse Show
Irish Antique Dealers Fair
Liffey powerboat racing, Dublin Regatta

**September** All-Ireland Football and Hurling Finals.

**October** Dublin City Marathon
Dublin Theatre Festival

**November** Irish National Stamp Exhibition

**December** Dublin Grand Opera Society Winter Season

AN EVENT · ROYAL DUBLIN SHOW

# Index

Main entries are shown in **bold**. Entries for places outside the city of Dublin generally refer to 'places of interest' listed in the Directory section.